How to Become
a Better Manager
in Social Work
and Social Care

Essential Skills for Social Work and Social Care Managers
Edited by Trish Hafford-Letchfield

Excellent management skills are an essential part of delivering services and play a key role in successful outcomes for service users. This series features short, accessible guides to the essential and everyday management skills involved in social work and social care management. The books consider the business aspects of management whilst retaining a focus on ethical practice, and include reader exercises, practical tools and useful frameworks.

other books in the series
Successful Project Management in Social Work and Social Care
Managing Resources, Assessing Risks and Measuring Outcomes
Gary Spolander and Linda Martin
ISBN 978 1 84905 219 1
eISBN 978 0 85700 460 4

How to Become
a Better Manager
in Social Work
and Social Care

Essential Skills for Managing Care

*Les Gallop and
Trish Hafford-Letchfield*

Jessica Kingsley *Publishers*
London and Philadelphia

Figure 2 based on Corey 2004 on p.48 is reproduced by permission of Dr Franklin Corey.
Table 3.1 based on Hay 2009 on p.60 is reproduced by permission of Sherwood Publishing.
Figure 4.1 from The Social Work Reform Board on p.83 is reproduced with the permission of the Controller of the HMSO and the Queen's Printer for Scotland.
Figure 6.1 from www.centreforwelfarereform.org on p.134 is reproduced by permission of The Centre for Welfare Reform.
Box 6.4 from Wright *et al.* 2006 on p.142 is reproduced by permission of Barnado's.
Box 5.1 and Box 6.6 on p.123 and p.146 are reproduced by permission of Christine Khisa.

First published in 2012
by Jessica Kingsley Publishers
73 Coller Street
London N1 9BE, UK
and
400 Market Street, Suite 400
Philadelphia, PA 19106, USA

www.jkp.com

Library of Congress Cataloging in Publication Data
Gallop, Les, 1946-
   How to become a better manager in social work and social care : essential skills for managing care / Les Gallop and Trish Hafford-Letchfield.
      p. cm. -- (Essential skills for social work and social care managers)
   Includes bibliographical references.
   ISBN 978-1-84905-206-1 (alk. paper)
   1. Social workers--Supervision of. 2. Social work administration. 3. Social service. I. Hafford-Letchfield,
Trish. II. Title.
   HV40.54.G35 2012
   361.0068--dc23
                                    2012001836

British Library Cataloguing in Publication Data
A CIP catalogue record for this book is available from the British Library

ISBN 978 1 84905 206 1
eISBN 978 0 85700 442 0

Trish dedicates this to the memory of Nasa Begum, feminist, activist, leader and dearest friend.

Les dedicates this to his brother and sisters – Jim, May (both now passed on), Doris, Mary and Betty – from their little brother. They give so much and take so little.

Contents

Tables, Figures and Boxes

Series Editor's Foreword

This book acknowledges the specific need for social work and social care managers to develop a wider portfolio of skills which embrace the business aspects of management alongside ethical practice in very demanding environments. Managers who I have worked with in different settings have often struggled with keeping up with new developments in management and particularly with having enough time to think about their own learning and professional development. Becoming skilful as a manager does not always naturally emerge from one's professional experiences although much of what we learn is generated from our experience and tacit knowledge. The need to develop more tailored or specific skills for successful management might come to your attention for the first time when you move into a new management role or when you make a transition from one management role to another. Managers often acquire responsibility for managing others without the benefits of formal management training, and resort to utilizing fundamental life skills combined with professional expertise and practice 'know-how'. This particular book, the first in the series of *Essential Skills for Social Work and Social Care Managers*, aims to give front line or aspiring managers access to a practical quality guide to some of these fundamental management skills. These have been particularly tailored for those working in social work and social care environments or any environment which has care at the core of its business.

The empirical evidence about the effectiveness of leadership and management development, what is taught on programmes and in the workplace, and its outcomes, is not very strong. There are well-documented tensions in introducing management and leadership theory into environments where uncertainty, turbulence and issues of inequality and power coexist. The literature of social work and social care is rich with critiques of the impact of managerialism and marketization on services. It is relatively scant, however, on how managers actually facilitate and promote more effective engagement of stakeholders in their day-to-day work. There is also insufficient knowledge in the field about social work managers' pivotal but challenging role in improving relationships within and between the organizations working together to provide more seamless, responsive and integrated services. This calls for the identification and acquisition of concrete tools that managers can use to promote their own learning. There is also a need for purposive fostering of organizational cultures in which self-managed learning can thrive, particularly given the increasing complexity of how services are delivered. This book aims to start with some basics in this respect by giving attention to skills that managers require in everyday practice, but with our unique context in mind. Managers need a tripartite framework when it comes to personal effectiveness; one which incorporates skills, knowledge *and* values. You will find that the authors always discus skills in the context of organizational structure and culture and refer to the conditions that foster learning and innovation specific to social work and social care.

There are a number of methods that in the workplace can be used to help assess and evaluate your skills. One of the unique features of this book is the multi-source feedback tool offered by the authors from the outset. They assert that we cannot learn skills merely by reading about them, but that managers have to be active in seeking feedback from those with a real stake in management development. Throughout this book the authors refer to numerous techniques for obtaining regular feedback from team members and other professionals. The activities and tools offered are aimed at encouraging you to build this into your normal management repertoire. These take into account the significant shift in the power and status of service users and carers, from traditional recipients of professional wisdom and judgements to one of co-producers and co-providers of care.

Developing management skills in social work and social care tends to be linked to national criteria or management standards. Whatever strategic architecture is developed, work-based and experiential learning remains a crucial method for developing and achieving both confidence and competence to make improvements. The topics in this book were chosen by the authors to address those fundamental skills that involve the application of knowledge to practice in a significant range of work activities, and in a variety of contexts. Whether they are complex or routine, most management activities require taking individual responsibility and exercising autonomy in the control or guidance of others as well as being a collaborative leader or member of a workgroup or team. These inherent tensions permeate each chapter.

The style of this book aims to be informal but draws on a sound knowledge base. Features of the book include:

- setting out the broader context for the skill being considered, including a summary of research findings

- 'On the Spot' activities which encourage you to reflect on the skill being discussed

- explaining practical tools that can be used in your management practice, demonstrated through direct application to a familiar case study

- a summary and action checklist for each area of skills discussed.

Each chapter is underpinned by the values and ethics of good management in social work and social care, drawing on the principles of distributed and participatory leadership. Management is a practical activity and this integrative task involves achieving synergy, balance and perspective. Most management activity also involves a continuous process of adaptation to changing pressures and opportunities in a complex political environment. There is a danger of overemphasizing technical knowledge and skills and neglecting the underpinning values and ethics that accompany our everyday communication with those around us. We also need to keep our eye on the broader structural issues and this book aims to help you make sense of these through its frequent references to the personal and democratic elements of management. These are essential to retain the professional nature of the work and the values inherent in social work and social care practice. Individual chapter topics include:

- exploring the concept of 'skill' and 'personal effectiveness' with a view to auditing and evaluating your current level of management skills

- managing and controlling your own time and the time of others, through methods of working which provide a firmer foundation for dealing with time management conflicts

- assessing and responding to change using a model to illustrate the different skills required to effectively manage change

- the skills required for planning staffing, recruiting and selecting colleagues

- examining and reflecting on the range of meetings that managers attend and the skills involved in setting personal service or organizational objectives for managing meetings and forums effectively

- the nature of relationships between managers and service users and the skills required to work in partnership with service users at different levels in the organization

- skilful negotiation and conflict management including informal and formal approaches when working with different parties

- effective mentoring and coaching skills in relation to workforce development and the challenges arising through changing patterns of migration, demography, policy directions and socio-economic circumstances.

Bryans and Mavin (2003, p.123) remind us that feeling like a manager is a 'complex balance between an individual's self-perception and the perception of others towards them, a fragile, dynamic and continual process easily threatened by one's own lack of confidence and the response of others'. Within the organizational setting this refers to the extent to which managers work collaboratively, and are mutually supportive and skilful in transferring knowledge between situations and people. Good quality management learning can ensure that managers provide support for their colleagues and find new ways of working and learning together. I hope you enjoy the challenge.

Trish Hafford-Letchfield
Series Editor

Acknowledgements

To Trish's parents Peter and Sylvia, son Ted and daughter Katie for their love and support and to her colleagues and friends; you know who you are! Special thanks go to Jacqui Saward and Karen Ridout, who always make me laugh at work.

Les would like to thank Scilla, Tom and Katy for all they give and for refusing to take him too seriously. He acknowledges past colleagues at Leicester and De Montfort Universities for both their patience and ideas, and wants to say a particular thanks to Rob, his co-mentor, from whom he has learned and still learns so much.

We appreciate what we have learned from the managers we have both worked with over the years. Our discussions and plans for this book are based on what they have told us about their everyday challenges in their management practice.

We are grateful to those who have granted us permission to reprint valuable materials. Every effort has been made to acknowledge sources of this work. Any notifications of omissions or errors in acknowledgements in this work are gratefully received.

Chapter 1

Becoming and Being an Effective Manager
Essential Skills and More

The loftiest towers rise from the ground.
Chinese proverb

Introduction

This chapter seeks to introduce you to the concept of skills within management practice. We begin with considering the notion of what it means to 'become' a manager and address some of the issues commonly faced by managers in social work and social care as they transition into new or different management roles. The acquisition of skills and knowledge in management is frequently cited by governments as the key to delivering a vision of quality services and the role managers have in shaping and changing services (Department for Children, Schools and Families (DCSF) 2009). Implementing policy requirements can involve the management of great complexity in different care settings. Many managers also work in managerialist regimes, which can impact on how one carries out the varied tasks of leading in an organization. These situations or environments have implications for how managers might learn and develop core knowledge and skills. This chapter will look at a number of concepts in relation to personal effectiveness and the notions of 'expertise' and 'skill' and will offer you a framework with which to audit your own management skills using a multi-source feedback tool based on some common leadership and management frameworks in social care. How we actually measure skill and its associated knowledge and values is generally an under-researched and under-documented area (Crisp *et al.* 2003; Cree and Macaulay 2001; Gould 2000) which is surprising given that management is essentially a practical activity and that managers use a very wide range of knowledge and skills within their practice.

Transitions into management and transferring skills

> On Friday, Gerry enjoyed his farewell party from the Duty Team in the Local Authority Children's Services, where for five years he had been a valued and increasingly knowledgeable practitioner. On Monday he arrived at his new job as a manager of a duty team in another office in another Local Authority. Whilst Gerry did his best to appear confident on the outside, he felt extremely anxious within. Rupa meanwhile attended her farewell party at the residential unit where she had been a highly trusted senior care assistant for four years. On Monday morning, she would be starting her new role as an assistant manager at another home for older people, but for the same private company. Neither of the new managers had slept too much the night before. Like a swan on the lake, they both were paddling furiously below, whilst above it appeared to be a picture of serenity.

Gerry's and Rupa's sleepless nights are a regular occurrence, when people in social work and social care move on from jobs in which they have developed competence and confidence, into new jobs where they sense that they may have to prove themselves all over again. On the positive side, both Rupa and Gerry were feeling enthusiastic about their new jobs: after all, their prospective employers had expressed enough confidence to appoint them, and they felt in need of the challenge. On the downside, no one quite knows how successfully their knowledge, skills and experience will travel and transfer to new environments. Enthusiasm and anxiety will thus tussle for prominence as people transfer to new roles, say their goodbyes to people they know well and hello to lots of new people, often unknown and in uncharted territory. Anita, a new manager of a community mental health team quoted in Reynolds *et al.* (2006, p.7) had a similar experience: 'I was probably quite good at what I did,' she wrote, 'but I have absolutely no guarantees whatsoever that I'm going to be any good as a manager.'

Very early on in their new roles, Rupa and Gerry discovered that this was a move which involved change at a number of levels. They knew it would feel more 'responsible' than before because they would have a wider range of duties; they knew it would be more about getting work done through delegation to others rather than doing it themselves. Less expected was the subtle change in identity. Before they had been 'one of us', included in work gossip and fun: now they were 'one of them', someone whose entry into a room seemed to cause a subtle change in atmosphere, despite their attempts to be personable and approachable. As this aspect of the promotion dawned on Gerry and Rupa, their confidence in their own skills and knowledge dropped for a while. 'One of them', perhaps, needs different skills from 'one of us'.

What the above familiar scenarios demonstrate is that people moving into new management roles in social work and social care find that management feels different from direct professional or care practice. Management learning involves bridging a gap where 'the whole range of attempts to cover learning including the narrower case of learning to manage' (Fox 1997, p.25). Fox (1997) also distinguishes between two different approaches to management learning: the first is *management education*, which is largely based on theoretical knowledge and associated with formal education; the second is *management development*, which is supported through workforce development, is more practical, and emphasizes a range of skills. Both are required to support the Social Work Task Force's assertion that 'skilled and confident front line managers are essential to good front line social work' (DCSF 2009, p.32). An apprentice manager may learn through a combination of the above approaches, although few may commence their management careers having completed a formal qualification or training in management. Traditional approaches to learning until recently emphasized cognitive methods, and tended to be individual. However, most emphasis in social work and social care is on the process of learning from experience, as a social activity embedded in its own social and cultural contexts (Hafford-Letchfield *et al.* 2008). Vygotsky (1978) claimed that all cognitive learning occurs at a social level before occurring at the individual level. Individual learning is therefore mediated by others with social interaction becoming an important component of learning. Lave and Wenger (1991) described learning as being situated in 'communities of practice', their term for how people learn naturally in their work communities. In the complex interagency, integrated and interdisciplinary environment of social work and social care, learning has roots in and interdependencies across its history, technology, developing work activity, career pathways and relations between old-timers and newcomers, managers and practitioners (Lave and Wenger 1991, p.61). Social learning therefore emphasizes practice over theory and the social over the individual, and it depends on tacit knowledge and embodied skills (Nonaka 1991). The topics in this book build on these assumptions about how managers learn skills. Most management skills will be applying what you already know in a different context. We will be encouraging you to think about the sorts of skills that managers like Rupa and Gerry need. As most social care organizations are not in the position to provide management development opportunities before people move into their first management positions, we hope that some of the topics will be of practical use to managers as they find their way in the sometimes turbulent world of social work and social care management. For more experienced managers, we hope that this book provides some useful ideas on the application of skills as they review their approach to, and effectiveness in, management.

What makes a manager effective?

Whilst we want to focus on skills, it would be foolish to suggest that managers become effective simply by developing their skills. Skills are necessary but not the whole story. So what else helps a manager to be effective? Pettinger (2001, p.1) argues that effectiveness in management requires the ability to:

- achieve things through people
- cope with uncertainty and change
- manage performance – identify levels of performance that are needed and then help develop people to achieve these.

Learning to become a manager is also a story of change. Bryans and Mavin (2003) in their study of women learning to be managers, for example, highlight the importance of acknowledging power and politics in organizations and how women need to work effectively through challenges to their value system and using their personalities in order to develop their identities as managers. Not all of these factors contributing to management learning are explicitly translated into occupational standards and we find the following standards in the UK (Skills for Care 2008b):

A. Managing self and personal skills.

B. Providing direction.

C. Facilitating change.

D. Working with people.

E. Using resources.

F. Achieving results.

These have been reproduced in a variety of documents in relation to social work and social care management standards:

- The induction standards for adult social care management use the same wording, but (importantly) add as a first standard: 'understanding the importance of promoting social care principles and values' (Skills for Care 2008a).

- The post-qualifying Leadership and Management Award (General Social Care Council 2010) is based on the same standards.

- The core and optional units for the NVQ Level 4 in Leadership and Management for Care Services cover more or less the same areas.

No one can rely just on skills to meet these standards. Social work and social care organizations have major differences to businesses, thus management theories, particularly those from a business orientation, may not always fit and therefore management development needs to actively incorporate the key elements outlined in Box 1.1.

Box 1.1: Five elements of an effective manager

1. Managers need *knowledge*. It is impossible to think, for example, of a retail sector manager moving into the management of a social work team with child protection responsibilities, or into a job managing residential care.

2. Managers need to *understand themselves* well enough to know what motivates them and what they struggle with: the 'perfect' manager exists only in the abstract. Our personal approach to work will contribute to our management style, which will in turn partly determine how we use (or do not use) our skills.

3. Managers need a strong *value base* from which they can ultimately judge their and others' performance. Moss (2007, p.3) puts it this way: 'without an awareness of values, our practice can become dangerous'.

4. Managers need to *understand their organizations*. No two organizations are alike. Rupa and Gerry will quickly discover the influence of the organization on how they perform. This will not just be the formal influence of policies and procedures. They will also experience, probably in a different way from before, the influence of the organization's 'culture'. Again we will return to this later in this chapter.

5. Lastly, managers need *skills* to make all of the other ingredients work: hence our interest in writing a book on skills in social care and social work management.

The centrality of values to effective management

Values ultimately give meaning and shape to management practice. The move from practice to the effective management of practice is one which can only be made if values continue to underpin thinking and behaviour. This is not a straightforward process, however, because, as Banks (2006) demonstrates, practice itself creates ethical dilemmas for practitioners, and these do not disappear with the move to management. Indeed sometimes they can seem amplified by the new context. The wide range of stakeholder groups and the potential conflict with each other as well as the endemic tensions between the needs of the individual, family and wider community, with the organization's resources and constraints requires managers to be looking both ways. The manager of practice is in a position not unlike Janus, the Roman god of doorways, passages and bridges, having to look both ways at once.

Lawler and Bilson (2010) assert the pervasive nature of ethical conduct in management practice where all behaviour in interaction with others has an ethical dimension because it changes the lives of those with whom we interact (p.168). They suggest that improvement in acting ethically requires giving attention to the emotional rather than the rational responses to situation through the vehicle of critical reflection. Their suggested approach to reflection on emotions is not the introspective one usually recommended, but focuses on awareness of emotion through physical states, actions and awareness of the other as they occur such as through drama, and other body-based learning techniques such as Alexander Technique and groupwork (p.170). Kouzes and Mico's 1979 analysis of 'domains' in public sector organizations is another means of explaining the sources of value tensions that managers of practice are likely to experience.

- The *policy* domain is concerned with the overall framework of the organization. It sits between the organization and the electorate. Here are politicians and senior managers, seeking to respond to external demands.

- The *management* domain is concerned with efficiency and effectiveness. It is hierarchical, and sits between the policy domain and the service domain. Managers have responsibility for ensuring that working arrangements are in place to meet service user needs.

- The *service* domain is concerned with the quality of service. It sits between the management domain and service users. Here are people who work directly with the agency's service users. This is the domain where most of the 'swamp' that Schön (1987, p.42) writes about, can be found. Schön is a well-known writer on critical reflective professional practice. He was prompted to consider how problems with uncertainties, anxieties and no easy solutions, encountered by practitioners and their managers in everyday situations, might be subsumed by those problems that have more obvious solutions.

Practice 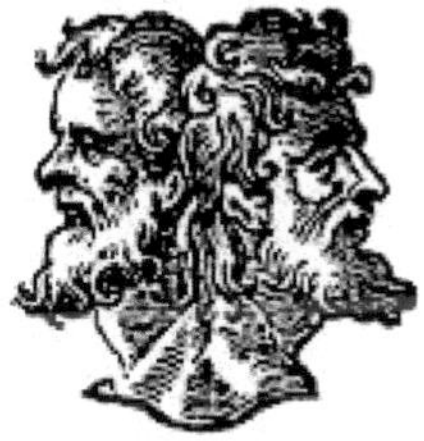   The organization

Figure 1.1: The manager as Janus

Each domain has its own values, some of which cross over between domains, some of which do not. Each has legitimacy, and Kouzes and Mico's central argument is that these domains necessarily coexist in some level of tension.

A sound value base is not enough by itself to ensure effective management in social work and social care. Consider two simple examples of this. A manager is deeply committed to inclusive practice. However, lacking skills in chairing meetings she fails to enable a service user to make a proper contribution, something we will discuss in more detail in Chapter 5. An opposite example makes the same point. A manager with sexist attitudes goes on a course about negotiation skills. The course is successful in its aims and objectives, and the manager learns new negotiation skills. When he returns to work, he may be a more effective negotiator technically...but his negotiations will still be underpinned by sexist attitudes with resultant problems in process and outcomes: disregarding women's contributions and ending up with an agreement which disadvantages women as service users. Skills are therefore an embedded component of learning and the vehicle through which the good intentions from our value base become managerial reality. Each needs the other in order for us to practise effective social care management. Self-awareness completes the ingredients for effective social work and social care management. Figure 1.2 illustrates our view of how all these ingredients interrelate, with values as central.

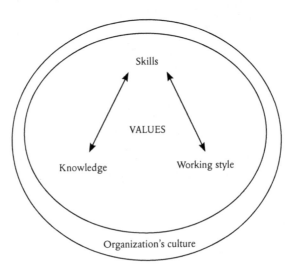

Figure 1.2: The effective social work and social care manager – Putting it all together

What do we mean by skills?

Given that this is a book about management skills, it seems sensible to pause for a moment and try to make sure that we are clear about what we mean when we talk about 'skills'. It is one of those words that we use all the time – and which we seldom stop and try to define. In the dictionary, skills are defined variously in terms of ability, expertise or ease in doing something. Immediately this suggests that skills will be displayed at differing levels. We would expect, for example, that an experienced social worker will operate at a higher skill level than one who is newly qualified. This is often discussed in terms such as 'novice' and 'expert', and a key factor at any stage of professional development is to consider the level of competency and skill alongside some predetermined framework for organizational and national standards in the relevant setting. Assessing different levels of skills also requires the use of multiple methods to assess and measure performance. Self-efficacy, again, is hard to measure yet important in developing a learner's own belief in their self-confidence and finding ways for this to be fostered. Some of the issues around skill are associated with positive psychology, and if this is not a factor in your local service culture it can have a negative impact on learners.

Expertise is generally used to describe someone whose practice encompasses artistry, creativity and critical thinking as opposed to sticking with more simple or linear and routine approaches. Some researchers have suggested that the ability to transfer learning from one situation to another is the hallmark of expertise, for example, the ability to coordinate the use of conceptual knowledge, specific skills and general procedures when confronting problematic situations (Benner 1984). The development of expertise is about being able to embed knowledge from different contexts and then to abstract and apply it to new situations or contexts, as exemplified in the challenge for both Gerry and Rupa. The transfer of learning requires structured support, guidance and facilitation from their own line managers, and other enabling people such as a coach or mentor. These people can help a novice manager articulate their assumptions and constructs and to make connections between these (Gould 2000). We will be looking at some of these issues in Chapter 8. Experts differ from novices in terms of the speed at which they might find a solution or develop a more intuitive grasp of certain situations. Experts tend to engage fully with a situation, are said to be more open to change and uncertainty and able to handle complexity.

It is common practice in the literature to distinguish between different sorts of skills. The most frequently made distinction is between 'hard' (sometimes called 'technical') and 'soft' skills (sometimes called 'core' or 'transferable' skills). The definitions used by Felstead, Gallie and Green (2002) in their analysis of the 2001 UK work skills survey are similar, with the addition of management skills. We have represented the rudiments of their definitions in Box 1.2.

Box 1.2: Defining different types of skills

Broad skills

These are measured by:

- the qualifications needed for the job

- the time taken to learn to do it well

- the length of prior training.

Generic skills

Skills that are used in varying degrees in all jobs, such as literary skills, number skills, communication, planning and problem-solving.

Particular skills

These might include reading long documents, identifying problems and careful listening to others.

Generic management skills

These skills are required in a variety of management jobs, and include coaching and motivating staff, controlling resources and thinking strategically.

Managers of course will need a mixture of all four. However, in social work and social care we would expect that effective practitioners will have already developed and fine-tuned a number of skills which should transfer into a management context. Our task will be to help you to evaluate your application of these in particular management contexts with a view to your determining the extent to which these skills are working effectively for you, your team, your service users and your organization. There may also be 'particular' skills that you need to work on to become effective as a manager.

All of this seems fairly straightforward, but discussion of skills is not without controversy. Social scientists remind us that skills are socially constructed, in that powerful groups can use their definition of skills (and their value) to further their interests. This is the subject of the film *Made in Dagenham*, released in 2010, about the struggle for equal pay of the Ford machinists in East London in the late 1960s. Not that the Equal Pay Act of 1970 has removed the gendered construction of skills. In social care, carers, in both home and residential settings, have been and are still mostly women, and front line caring is defined by not only its pressures and increasingly complex demands but also by its low pay. In their study of nursery nurses, Findlay, Findlay and Stewart (2009) found a sharp difference between the commonly held public stereotypes about their work and the reality. They concluded that the caring aspect of their work (closely associated with mothering and construed as 'natural' and therefore lowly valued) overshadowed the educational contributions they made: and it is the educational aspects that would have increased their standing in wider society. The result of this gendered view of these workers was that they earned less than the national average wage. Cockburn's research (1983) also uncovered the impact of gender on how skills are perceived in the printing industry. Here she found that in the older industry arrangements, where men were compositors, they had been recognized as 'skilled labour', and women, employed as typists, as 'unskilled'. When new technology was brought in, compositing was no longer required – replaced by typing – and the men faced a contradiction in how they saw themselves and the women with whom they had worked. Now needing to develop and use typing ('female') skills, they had either to see themselves as unskilled or to acknowledge that the women were as skilled as they were. This analysis extends beyond gender to any area where some groups have the power to determine the value of skills. Novelist Joseph Heller in *Catch 22* (1955) captured the class basis of this when he described a character, Orr, as having 'a thousand valuable skills that would keep him in a low income group all his life' (Heller 1994, p.397).

This view of skills as being socially constructed points us towards the importance of:

- critical analysis as we explore skills in a social work and social care management context

- understanding structural power differentials if we are to use our skills in the promotion of greater equality in employment.

It does not deny the importance of skill development, however, and we now turn to some of the more practical challenges in developing and fine-tuning our management skills.

Developing management skills and personal effectiveness

To develop skills and apply them in particular management contexts, we need:

- to audit and reflect upon our current level of skills against the relevant standards or frameworks for social work and social care

- an understanding of 'what works' – what effective practice looks like (e.g. what helps to make a negotiation successful)

- from this, access to frameworks that might be useful in carrying out responsibilities in that area (e.g. models of change management)

- opportunities to practise the skills

- sufficient self-awareness to know what helps or gets in the way when we apply skills in practice

- time and space for reflection on our performance, perhaps supported by self-assessment

- feedback from trusted others.

This view of how we develop skills has informed our approach to this book. You will see that we have tried in each chapter to give you access to some of the key literature on each topic; to provide some frameworks which should be of use in applying your skills to that area of management; and to give you opportunities for self-assessment, including attention to personal working styles. The remainder of this chapter will return to two areas touched on in Box 1.1: first, the importance first of knowing yourself and second, the importance of understanding the organization in which you work. We have argued that these have a part to play in determining how effective managers are. We will complete this chapter by providing you with an opportunity to audit your own skills.

Knowing oneself well enough

The last two decades or so have been marked by the rise and rise of 'managerialism', an approach to management that emphasizes the hierarchical nature of organizations, through which statements almost like mantras developed about 'the manager's right to manage'. Consistent with this is the focus on top-down targets and objectives, and management as 'command and control' (Clarke and Newman 1997; Harris 1998; Jones 2001; Lymbery 2001). We might see this as a corrective to earlier laissez-faire approaches to management, but managerialism has been criticized for its neglect of the importance of the people side of organizations. Related to this is Hafford-Letchfield's (2009) observation that such an approach privileges administrative requirements over reflective practice. In human resources terms, managerialism has been more interested in the 'resource' than in the 'human' and resources can neither feel nor reflect.

Social care and social work managers ignore the person at their peril, given that the work of their staff is essentially about people and their aspirations and struggles. The 'personal' is therefore (or should be) a central component in their work. Bowen and Schneider (1988) reinforce this from their research evidence on service organizations:

- Their products are largely intangible, and 'customers' will judge them through impressions. The Community Mental Health Team receptionist will be judged by interpersonal qualities such as friendliness.

- 'Production' and 'consumption' are simultaneous – the act of providing home care, for example, coincides necessarily with the receipt of it by the service user. Judgements of the service will go across a range of personal reactions, including what the service user takes into the interaction – 'Can I trust him?' 'Is he going to take over?' and so on.

- The 'customer' actively participates in the process. Sometimes, of course, this might be an undermining of it, as in the parent who is suspected of abusing a child and who refuses to allow a medical examination.

We make these points here because they show the limits in applying industrial models of management to social care and social work. They also act as a powerful reminder that social care management is about people and their feelings – including our own. This has important implications for us as we seek to develop and apply skills in management; such efforts might be thwarted if we lack self-awareness, an awareness of what makes us tick as people. A number of commentators on management stress this. For Furze and Gale (1996), for example, 'the starting point in developing managerial effectiveness must lie in developing our understanding, not only of the way other people behave and interact, but of ourselves'. Without this, they argue, 'the unthinking application of otherwise valuable management techniques will flounder on the rocks of ignorance' (p.5). In other words we cannot manage people without managing ourselves and we cannot manage ourselves without understanding ourselves. In their illuminating study of the realities of leadership, Binney, Wilke and Williams (2005) see self-awareness as the means through which we can understand and exert control over our 'demons', rather than as a way of getting rid of them. They see these demons as the worries and insecurities left over from earlier life experiences, and to these authors they are what make each of us unique. In their view the art of leadership lies in understanding, not changing, ourselves: 'if people can understand their demons and appreciate them for their positive, as well as negative, impact, it helps them to be successful leaders' (p.76).

These ideas are central to recent research about the relationship between successful management and 'emotional intelligence'. The concept of emotional intelligence originates from the 1970s, but was popularized by Goleman in 1996. Central to the idea is that traditionally defined intelligence does not always help us to explain why some people are more effective in dealing with life's pressures and in becoming successful. According to its supporters, *emotional* intelligence is what makes the difference. The main features of emotional intelligence are:

- self-awareness
- other awareness
- self-management
- relationship management.

Both Morrison (2007) and Howe (2008) link emotional intelligence to effectiveness in social work. Unsurprisingly, emotional intelligence has begun to interest writers on management and there is evidence linking high scores on emotional intelligence with effectiveness in management

(Gardner and Stough, 2002; George 2000; Goleman 1998). We are persuaded by these arguments and want therefore to make a link with self-awareness in this book on skills. In thinking about self-awareness, we refer to a model derived from Transactional Analysis (TA), the focus of a book – *Working It Out at Work* – by Julie Hay (2009). TA has its critics, who point, for example, to the relative lack of an empirical base. What we want to stress about the application of this framework when thinking about skills, is that we do not see it as offering 'truths' about ourselves and others. There is a real danger in any instruments designed to explore psychological processes that we end up with labels that simplify and deny the importance of both context and personal growth. We think that the TA model, however, provides a starting point with insights into the human condition and into relationships between people and is one useful reflection point as you consider your own approach as a manager. There are other models that will be incorporated into the text as we move through the different skill areas outlined in the chapter of this book.

The central idea behind Hay's working styles is that our approach to work is influenced by 'drivers'. These are similar to the 'demons' referred to above and have a basis in earlier life experiences, particularly how we were parented. There are five such drivers, described in TA terms as:

1. I will be OK if I am *perfect*.

2. I will be OK if I am *strong*.

3. I will be OK if I *hurry up*.

4. I will be OK if I *please you*.

5. I will be OK if I *try hard*.

Let us take one example of these and their relationship to earlier experiences of being parented. The driver to 'be perfect' is thought to have its origins in a style of parenting in which nothing the child does is good enough – so that the child has to keep on trying to do things better to gain the parental approval that might never really come. The driver for the adult therefore is always to try for perfection. Table 1.1 summarizes the five working styles as described by Hay.

Table 1.1: Characteristics of working styles

Working style	Advantages...	The downside...
Be perfect	Everything must be exactly right, so that work is accurate, reliable, to a very high standard. Well organized and planned. Have contingency plans. Projects run efficiently.	Deadlines sometimes missed because of too much checking for mistakes. Get too concerned with details. Sometimes reports will have too much information. Find it hard to delegate because of not trusting others to work to our standards.
Be strong	Good in crises and when under pressure. Can be relied on to keep logical when others are starting to panic. Stay emotionally detached and so make difficult decisions without feeling bad.	Hard to admit to worries or shortcomings, and so find it hard to ask for help. Can end up with too much work. Others can find detachment hard to deal with. Can be hard to get to know.
Hurry up	Work quickly, get a lot done. Good with short deadlines. Pressure gives energy. Getting things done quickly makes us feel good. Not much time spent in preparation.	Jobs left until deadlines get short. Hurrying leads to more mistakes. Quality may suffer. Can seem impatient, finish other people's sentences for them.
Please people	Good team members. Real interest in others. Good to have around because of empathy and understanding. Work hard at getting team closer together. Sensitive to others' feelings.	Avoid any risk of upsetting others, and reluctant to challenge even when challenge is needed. Hesitant to state own views assertively. Can take even constructive criticism badly.
Try hard	Enthusiastic. Good at getting things going. Often will volunteer for new tasks or cases. Will pay attention to all aspects of the task.	More committed to trying than succeeding. Enthusiasm wanes fairly quickly. Can be resented for doing the exciting, early parts but leaving the rest for others. Completion can be a problem.

Source: adapted from Hay 2009

Is it possible to find yourself and colleagues in these descriptions? Hay argues that, while we might find bits of all of these in ourselves, we will typically have one or two dominant styles.

From understanding ourselves to understanding our organizations

We want to move now from the process of understanding what drives us from inside at work to what influences us from the outside. Writers and researchers on organizations have become increasingly interested since the 1980s in what is commonly known as the 'culture' of organizations. To demonstrate this popularity: a short time searching for 'organizational culture' on www.amazon.co.uk late in 2010 yielded 5317 results. Although seen as important in the analysis of contemporary organizations, Mannion et al. (2008) argue that we can trace some interest in it as far back as 431 BC!

When we focus on culture, we do so in contrast to focusing on structures. It is by no means a simple concept: like a slippery bar of soap in the shower, you can think that you have grasped it but suddenly lose it it. Mannion et al. (2010) undertook some research into the changing nature of management cultures in the NHS and the impact that organizational culture has on organizational performance. Based on three case studies, they identified commonalities across various approaches to culture and argued that the study of what organizational members and groups share within a culture relates to three areas (Mannion et al. 2010, p.12). First, they found beliefs, values, attitudes and norms of behaviour, where there is shared thinking. Second, they referred to symbols in the organization such as typical routines or traditions. Third, they identified unspoken assumptions that can be recognized in how stories are told and how people make sense of them.

An often quoted definition is simply 'the way we do things round here'. Egan, a theorist known for his work in psychotherapy and author of a seminal social work text *The Skilled Helper* (1994), makes a powerful contribution to the debate on culture when he argues that all organizations have two sides. First, they have a public face that has official statements and will probably include mission statements, agency aspirations and annual reports. Second, they have a 'shadow side'. This is the side of the organization that does not appear in any public statements. It is the side where, for example:

- norms of behaviour are established

- power struggles happen

- emotions are located and expressed.

This suggests an organizational picture as in Figure 1.3. You will note the overlap between the shadow side and Mannion *et al.*'s view of culture. The two sides of the organization coexist and both impact on individual and collective performance. The public side, by definition, is much more accessible to outsiders.

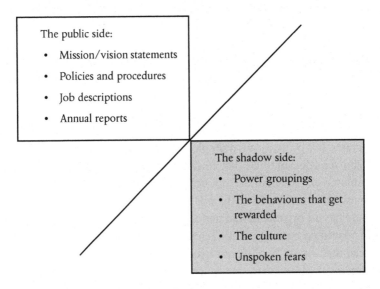

The public side:

- Mission/vision statements

- Policies and procedures

- Job descriptions

- Annual reports

The shadow side:

- Power groupings

- The behaviours that get rewarded

- The culture

- Unspoken fears

Figure 1.3: The two sides of organizations

Egan sees culture as being the most powerful part of the shadow side. Hafford-Letchfield's experience supports such a view (2009). She argues, for example, that reorganizations are more likely to be effective if they acknowledge the influence of culture. For her, therefore, actively trying to understand, monitor and influence the culture in your organization is time well spent by any manager.

Auditing your skills

Having conceptualized what we mean when we talk about skills, this final section offers a framework for auditing your own skills using a tailored multi-source feedback tool. This tool was developed by Hafford-

Letchfield for use with various leadership and management programmes she has been involved with in higher education over a number of years and her activity in helping managers to audit their own skills informed her initial interest in contributing to this book. Moreover, formal evaluation of the activities involved in managers undertaking an audit of their own level of skills has demonstrated that seeking multi-source feedback has great merit when designing an individual learning and development plan (Hafford-Letchfield and Bourn 2011). Managers need concrete tools to assess and promote their own learning. The tool introduced here is designed to give learner managers increased autonomy, choice and control as well as introducing components of flexibility into their learning process. The tool is essentially made up of different questionnaires aimed at seeking specific feedback from partners and stakeholders in management practice. These tools can be found in the Appendix for ease of access with further instructions on how to use them.

Becoming active in seeking feedback from one's own line manager, peers, staff, colleagues from different disciplines or agencies and service users and carers, can promote a more shared understanding about the skills and competencies necessary and desirable to achieve an equal partnership in management development. According to Skinner, Saunders and Beresford (2004), it is also more likely to lead to more meaningful change as it opens up debate about us all being on a learning journey. Investment in this type of model also invites your own line manager and colleagues to share responsibility for identifying learning opportunities in the workplace so that skills development can be aligned with your practice realities. The multi-source feedback tool provided in the Appendix is relatively easy to use and was based on assessing those six key areas relating to common leadership and management skills in social care referred to earlier in the chapter (Skills for Care 2008a):

- managing self and personal skills
- providing direction to others
- facilitating change
- working with people
- using resources
- achieving results.

Each questionnaire can be used as a standalone or you may wish to adapt or personalize it in the design of your own questionnaire. For example, you could use the 'questionnaire for staff' to get feedback from your staff on your supervision and communication skills in the team. Alternatively you can use all five questionnaires or in a combination of two, three or four together. The greater the number of sources of feedback, the more rounded and whole process of assessment and evaluation will be obtained. The process is illustrated in Figure 1.4.

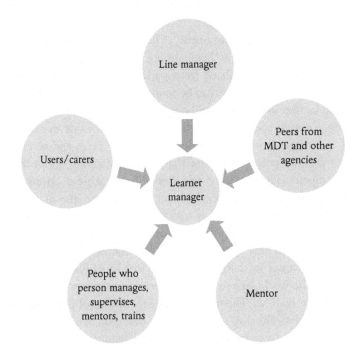

Figure 1.4: The multi-source feedback process

By engaging in auditing and evaluating your own management skills, you will be taking up opportunities for critically reflective practice together with an appreciation of the impact of management communication with those we manage. This is particularly challenging in asking service users and carers about how they perceive and see us (for further discussion see Chapter 6) as well as thinking about how we might make use of mentoring and coaching skills which can support those areas of development that emerge from the process (see Chapter 8). Using the tool encourages us to set our own goals for learning and to exploit everyday experiences in the workplace as potential learning opportunities. Further guidance on how to use the tool is contained in the introduction to the Appendix. By means of an overview this involves:

1. Seeking feedback from a range of stakeholders in your management practice. The tool encourages you to utilize Likert scale ratings ('seldom', 'sometimes', 'quite often', 'often' or 'always') which are then numerically scored and collated. It also invites comments about performance in each area of your skill development, derived from the national leadership and management standards. These are not based on scientific inquiry but aim to provide helpful indicators in the relevant areas.

2. Assessing and evaluating the feedback in terms of the whole picture using the scoring process provided. This overall picture can be used to inform discussion with your line manager and/or mentor to develop an analysis of strengths revealed and to identify areas for further development. You are also encouraged to rank the relative importance of each skill to your own work environment and role in the organization so that any development is linked to the needs or the organization and its business plan. Here you will be making a link to your current role and responsibilities.

3. Drawing up an individual learning and development plan within which specific areas are prioritized for attention alongside the identification of learning opportunities to facilitate these through work-based learning.

4. Using the tools again at a future date to review progress and set further goals.

The use of multi-source feedback systems has become widespread in management development and they work best when integrated into other sources of evaluation. Using this tool does, however, need careful preparation and transparent guidance about the process so that those giving the feedback understand the purposes and use of feedback given. You may, for example, wish to be mindful of who you approach for feedback, since what is required is constructive feedback. Seeking feedback proactively builds on the premise that one can have more control over getting feedback and be in a position to respond to it by giving up control and allowing others to have a voice (Hafford-Letchfield and Bourn 2011).

This is a unique consideration in multi-source feedback techniques and the key to facilitating one's own learning. For Gerry and Rupa, for example, it would be a good starting point in their new management roles and also validate their existing skills and areas of strength.

Chapter summary

This chapter has provided a general overview of the importance and significance of management skill within its context. You have been introduced to some of the key theories about learning in relation to skill development and encouraged to make opportunities to get feedback from those you relate to in order to assess your own personal effectiveness and to identify areas for development. We have tried to illustrate the place of skills in management, arguing that they enable managers to apply their knowledge and to convert the good intentions of their value base into positive outcomes in 'real' organizations. The remainder of this book considers some of the more common demands on managers' skills. These are not typical of areas found in leadership and management textbooks in social work and social care. We have also written them in a way that enables each chapter to be more or less self-contained. Following your own audit, you may wish to be selective and go direct to those chapters that are of particular relevance to you at this moment in time.

Action checklist

1. How does the current context for your service determine the skills you require? Are there any new areas of skill development that need to be addressed or updated?

2. When was the last time you paid attention to your own development as a manager? How does discussion about your skills influence your own supervision and appraisal process?

3. How will you get feedback on your personal skills? Do you need to undertake a formal audit or seek feedback?

Chapter 2

Managing Yourself and Managing Others

There's Never Enough Time in the Day

We are what we repeatedly do.
Excellence, then, is not an act, but a habit.
Aristotle

Introduction

Time is probably our most precious (and most undervalued) resource, and taking control of how we use our time merits special attention. The variety of tasks that managers of social work and social care do and the integral nature of time management requires us to constantly review and improve our time management skills. Time management is a fundamentally important task for managers. Managing and controlling your time may contribute to keeping up your own morale, as well as being able to stimulate and maintain the morale of others you work with. Stress is among the main causes of employee absence (MacDonald 2005) and we now have a number of policy documents and guidance that emphasize the importance of managing well-being at work (Department of Health 2004). This might, for example, be through the provision of timely and high quality supervision and planning, which in turn increases reliability and provides opportunities for good communication. As managers, people look to us for support in managing their work and we are expected to be able to 'multi-task' whilst remaining in control. In spite of our best efforts, however, not having the right structures or resources in place can leave us at the mercy of random events. Even with the best laid plans, because of the nature of the work that we do it might only take one or two crises for chaos to ensue. Feeling as comfortable as we can in managing these scenarios might be the best we can realistically achieve. This can be done by ensuring that our methods of working provide us with a firm foundation for dealing with potential time management conflicts.

This chapter looks at the different and interrelated skills involved in this area. We encourage managers to review how they use their time by drawing on a number of models for prioritizing and using this precious resource effectively. There will be a balance in the chapter between motivational and philosophical drivers, both intrinsic and extrinsic. We will also consider some of the more practical management tools that can help us to 'get more organized', where the latter reflects a more common approach to time management. We will touch on the psychological or emotional content of managers' relationships with those who make regular or frequent demands on their time. Specific topics will include how to work with priorities within the context of organizational culture, building on some of the systemic literature on organizations (Huffington *et al.* 2004). This refers to issues around organizational and team cultures which can cause rigidity and inflexibility in responding to problems in a timely fashion. We will be introducing concepts that are further developed in subsequent chapters, such as making use of delegation and running effective meetings (see Chapter 5) as well as handling conflict (see Chapter 7). You will be introduced to some practical tools for time management based on realistic scenarios in care settings. Some of the benefits and issues of using technology, given the increasing emphasis on IT systems in social work and social care, will also be explored. This chapter is underpinned by a distributed and participative leadership approach which recognizes the role of professional autonomy. Participative leadership values the contribution of others through their different roles and is integral to time management as it facilitates their engagement in achieving both short and long term objectives. As you progress through the chapter we will capture some key lessons about time management for you to reflect upon later.

But I haven't got time to manage my time!

Let's start with the example of Dominique Dinh who manages 'Lotus', a resource centre for carers, contracted by the local authority to provide support services. Lotus is moving towards offering more personalized support for carers with personal budgets and direct funding. Dominique works within a very flat management structure where as the chief executive she plays a number of roles including the direct supervision of six staff, premises management and business development of the organization. Dominique is an informal carer herself. On some days she feels as if she is going to 'crack up' although her staff would never know it! Being very involved with day-to-day operational issues means she is falling badly behind with more strategic developments and major report writing. She cannot remember the last time she stopped for lunch and is fed up with taking work home. Nine times out of ten this is unsuccessful because once home, she has no energy to tackle it. Dominique knows that if she does not take a break soon, her health may be at risk, yet there are so many people relying on her. Whilst she has always been 'a good reliable manager' for staff and service users, the external demands on the organization to secure funding and develop innovative services are taking over her 'day job'.

Dominique's situation may not be untypical, and illustrates some common dilemmas of managing time for managers in social work and social care. Good use of time is implicitly linked to issues around productivity and quality, exemplified in devising initiatives to reduce turnaround times and improve the execution of assessments and service provision in order to get more value for money. Her actions also reflect tendencies towards procrastination which we discuss later on in the chapter. Dominique's work exhibits time-related restrictions and time-bounded activities and processes with deadlines for completion or review.

Consequently, there is an 'invest to save' imperative within the core role of managers and the workflows they control. Whilst managers in social work and social care have been delegated increased responsibility, growing surveillance and perceived control over the activities that professionals undertake has led to additional pressure in the workplace (Hafford-Letchfield 2010). Whilst most carers and staff may think that Lotus is doing a fantastic job, this might only be demonstrated through the performance information provided to the local authority in line with contract conditions. At the same time Lotus needs to expand and find new business in the changing context of personalization. Dominique is experiencing a typical time famine (Perlow 1999) where she not only lacks *physical* time to deal with the different demands on it, but the *quality* of her time, if it remains poor, will ultimately impact on the effectiveness of longer term outcomes for Lotus.

There has been minimal research into workload management, workflow management and management of time in social work and social care although a lot has been said about its effects on practice (Munro 2011). The literature tends to document those issues concerned with the impact of bureaucratization (Burton and van de Broek 2008; Dustin 2007) and more recently the impact of new technologies on professional practice (Ceeney 2009; Holmes *et al.* 2009; Weinburg *et al.* 2003). Productivity and multi-tasking are integral to effective use of time. For example, you may be reading this chapter whilst doing something else such as travelling to a meeting, or with the radio on in the background. This is known as a polychromic approach. A monochromic approach is where the task takes up your full attention. You may be solely focused on reading this chapter to the exclusion of any other activities in order to maximize your attention span. The approach required is related to the quality of the task. Being aware of your own attitudes, values and personal capabilities about time is an important precursor to managing it for others as, according to Forster (2006, p.122), 'you will never get anyone to attach a higher priority to your work that they perceive you are giving to it yourself'.

The context for attitudes, beliefs and values underpinning time management

Thinking about organizational and team well-being and motivation is linked to confronting issues about time management. It goes hand in hand with staff being supported to undertake meaningful and challenging work with opportunities to apply their knowledge and skills. This should take place within effective working relationships with managers, colleagues and service users in a safe and healthy environment. It is particularly important for staff to achieve personal aspirations and a work–life balance; something which Dominique (see the case study on the previous page) is obviously lacking. Perhaps one of the most important factors in employees' well-being is in the relationships they will have with you their line manager, and your ability to recognize the volume or complexity of work to make sure it is not too much for them as team members. The tendency to obscure issues and be seen 'to cope' has been cited in enquiries (Laming 2009). Poor management is also related to staff retention in social work and social care (Cornes *et al.* 2010a; Harris, Manthorpe and Hussein 2008). Both issues are extremely costly. According to systems theory, developing a working hypothesis that informs how you bring what is unknown, unattended, or unconscious in staff day-to-day work, can also shed new light on the actual challenges that they are facing. Formulating a working hypothesis may open up fresh and sometimes unexpected avenues for decision and action; in negotiating and managing change, handling conflict, rethinking work structures or crafting vision and strategy (Huffington *et al.* 2004). In summary, there are essential factors leading to personal and organizational well-being which will have an impact on processing and progressing more valuable outcomes. According to Kraybill (2003) these factors may include:

- Creating an environment in which values, ethics and management style are acknowledged and given time and attention.

- Providing opportunities for frequent open communication and dialogue.

- Giving attention to team working and cooperation, including peer support.

- Providing clarity and unity of purpose about the work being undertaken.

- Considering flexibility and discretion and giving support for reasonable risk taking.

- Recognition that people need a balance between their work and personal life and an opportunity to regularly recharge their batteries.

- The ability to negotiate workload and the pace of work without fear of reprisals or punishment.

- Being fairly compensated for the work in terms of salary, opportunities for career development and progression and other benefits.

Clarity of roles

Role conflict can occur for individuals such as Dominique if new expectations of her role go unacknowledged following changes from external demands. Managing role expectation is a vital element in maintaining a role system within an organization. Subsequent ambiguity in her role may arise where she is expected to spend more time on strategic developments, yet spend the same amount of time managing day-to-day operational issues. The tensions for managers in having to look both ways were referred to in Chapter 1. Lack of acknowledgement of role ambiguity combined with work overload is likely to lead to Dominique experiencing a lack of confidence and perhaps deterioration in her interpersonal relationships. According to Handy (1999) a positive approach would involve regular review of organizational goals and targets with team and individuals, and the reallocation of roles and responsibilities in relation to abilities, potential and the needs of the organization. Dominique could perhaps make better use of her trustees between board meetings by drawing on their valuable knowledge and skills in some of the more pressing areas of strategic planning. With such a responsible role and a flat support structure, Dominique is probably apprehensive about revealing the pressures she is under. Asking for help may be perceived as a weakness. This is the working style discussed in Chapter 1 that Hay (2009) describes as 'Try Hard'. Over-preoccupation with external pressures such as outsourcing, target setting and performance management may also rub up against any emphasis on innovation and creativity. Dominique needs to find ways of facilitating creativity within her organization as well as to use her political skills and know-how to influence future decisions and actions.

Thinking about time from a 'systems' perspective

Taking a systems approach to being effective with one's time is not just a matter of physically getting things done, but involves several stages in which you are able to recognize changes impacting on the organization and their subsequent demands on the workforce (Huffington et al. 2004). Anticipating and acting on change is an essential management skill as we will see in the next chapter. Time management involves building in opportunities for clarifying and understanding the nature of issues confronting the organization and being able to articulate these clearly. These are issues concerned with the *quality* of time management. Dominique needs to use her staff, service users and trustees in questioning and probing to develop how other people understand and describe the demands being faced by the organization so that she literally does not have to take the work home. If Dominique adopted a systems approach, she would feel able to analyse the issues and engage her team in generating potential solutions. The pressure to 'be strong', as we saw in Table 1.1, will also move Dominique away from achieving a more distributed or participative leadership style. These are skills related to change management, the subject of our next chapter. Having considered the bigger picture, we will continue with looking at some practical tools and techniques in organizing one's time.

Practical workload and time management systems

Up until now we have been looking at some psychological and sociological aspects of time management which establish the basis for how we manage ourselves. One of the messages is that both individual and group well-being are key to working collaboratively, which in turn forms the foundation for using resources such as time effectively. In practical terms, any workload management system needs to incorporate the following:

- mechanisms or triggers in place which flag up any time management issues so that steps can be taken to find solutions

- staff being managed need accurate information about the timescales expected, the different priorities and deadlines for particular tasks and, most importantly, support to be able to manage their own workload

- capacity has to be built into the team or service's systems so that any exceptional demands on time can be responded to in order to regain control of workflow or time needed

- some sort of feedback system where information about how time allocated for particular work can be used to improve the system further as well as to inform future service needs and for planning (business process re-engineering is the term used to refer to the analysis and design of workflows and processes within an organization).

These latter two aspects are generally captured through measurement or documentation of the activity of individuals and teams. Much has been written about the prescriptive timescales in social work and social care (Laming 2009; Munro 2011) which, whilst seemingly related to responding to service users needs, or the throughput of work, have become overstandardized. These have come about following legitimate concerns about 'drift' in cases where service users might be at risk and as tools for rationing the use of resources and for increasing accountability. However, the over-preoccupation with meeting timescales may obscure issues about the actual quality of activities that staff are engaged in. This can create a punitive climate in which we manage in order to meet timescales and lose sight of our original purpose. Time can only be calculated precisely within highly structured environments or tasks, but these are not always predictable within the nature of the work that we do. This is where experience and flexibility come into play, including our individual approach and knowledge of our own and others' abilities.

Find out what you do: assessing your current time management

You are invited in this section to participate in a series of exercises designed to enable you to reflect on what issues are confronting your current time management. As a starting point you should plot how you currently spend your time to identify the areas that need attention. The first exercise, completing Table 2.1, might seem tedious or obvious, but is important as it is designed to find out your base line for testing how you determine your own work priorities.

You can make the intervals larger or smaller to suit the type of environment you work in and the pace and variety of work. If you work at home, in the evenings, or weekends, include these in your table so that you get a real feel for the amount of time you spend on work activity. If you can do this over a whole week, the exercise will be even more informative.

Table 2.1: 'On the Spot' – Logging management activities

Date:				
	Activities			
Time	**Meeting**	**Supervision**	**Email**	**Other**
09.00				
09.30				
10.00				
10.30				
11.00				
11.30				

Reflecting on the completed audit could include some interrogation of how much of your time is ordered, or about order, and how much of your time involves creative activities. Forster (2006) asserts that the qualities of being creative, ordered and effective depend very closely on each other. Effectiveness is a measure of how far the order in your working life allows your creativity to express itself and is the difference between action and activity. Being very busy does not mean you are effective and requires a workable plan to change your methods and approach (Forster 2006). His formula – 'effectiveness = creativity and order' – reveals that effectiveness is the difference between action and activity and one needs to take real action to be effective. For example, applying his formula to your audit might mean that you score 6 out of 10 for creativity and 5 out of 10 for order, giving you a score of 30 per cent effectiveness (6×5). The aim would then be to increase those activities that bring order to your work. Lymbery (2003) has commented on the constraints placed on creativity and reflection in social work practice by factors such as high workloads, time and the need to respond quickly to circumstances. He suggests that practice is located on a continuum which encompasses both competence and creativity, and is determined by the level of predictability and the complexity of the situation. Care practitioners are constantly confronted with situations not amenable to concrete forms of resolution, and require individual responses and the application of 'professional artistry' (Schön 1987). Insights into the level of creativity in one's work can help to reframe the nature of these relationships between order, competence and creativity.

Developing effective habits

We are now going to introduce you to the work of Covey (Covey 2004; Covey, Merrill and Merrill 1994). In his popular work *The 7 Habits of Highly Effective People* (2004), Covey developed a 'time management matrix' which, he argued, enables us to achieve confidence and balance in doing well what matters most. We have contextualized his matrix below, which aims to describe how we spend our time under four key categories:

1. Working on *important and urgent* tasks such as responding to crisis situations with service users and meeting significant deadlines such as external reporting and timely delivery of services.

2. Working on *important but non-urgent* tasks and being proactive, such as developing strategy and business plans, budget planning, developing prevention and consultation strategies, responding to complaints and quality issues, and learning and staff development and support activities.

3. Working on *less important and non-urgent* activities, for example, attending to routine emails and meetings, responding to enquiries, seeking, giving and evaluating information, dealing with interruptions, networking and special interest activities.

4. Working on *unimportant and unnecessary* tasks, for example, trivia, personal emails and undertaking activities which primarily give pleasure.

Earlier we referred to public enquiries into failures of professional social work practice and subsequent debates about workload in social work. A comprehensive study (Baginsky *et al.* 2010) examined workloads, supervision and other factors impacting on front line social work practitioners and social work provision in local authority adult and children services, as well as private, voluntary and independent agencies. Almost half of the respondents were reported to be working more than their contracted hours, with 9 per cent working over nine additional hours per week. Overall user-related work accounted for about 73 per cent of time including case-related recording and case-related work in the social workers' agencies and with other professionals. Complaints centred on technical problems, lack of accessibility of reports for service users, repetition and limited scope for flexibility and analysis, particularly in relation to ICT systems. Covey's approach to time management above aims to support the achievement of effectiveness by aligning oneself to a system of priorities (Covey 2004). His approach goes beyond task lists towards attributing values, primary roles and principles when deciding which activities are most important, so that decisions are not merely determined by time or urgency but have a compass of purpose and values.

Figure 2.1 demonstrates Covey's 2×2 matrixes where tasks are classified as 'urgent' and 'non-urgent' on one axis and 'important' or 'non-important' on the other. Items in quadrant 2 are those we are likely to neglect. These are, however, central to being effective given that they will help us work towards longer term goals. These might include preventative strategies which are often neglected in social care or under-resourced. Timely and quality staff supervision can be another area that contributes towards longer term goals, particularly in relation to staff satisfaction and retention. Covey recommends identifying important items by focusing on a few key priorities and roles which will vary from person to person and which can be broken down into small goals for each role in order to achieve a more holistic balance in managing work. Delegation (as we shall see in Chapter 5) is an important aspect of time management as it focuses on results and benchmarks agreed in advance rather than on prescribing detailed work plans. Again, within social care, this is illustrated in the arguments about professional autonomy and accountability (Munro 2011).

Using the information from your audit in Table 2.1, try to plot 'what you do' against Covey's four categories described above. These are visually represented in Figure 2.1. You may wish to first colour code your content in Table 2.1 by coding your activities to correspond with one of four colours allocated to each quadrant. Make a note of what you discovered about where your priorities are when organizing your work. It might also be useful for you and your supervisor to discuss together what you found out about the strategic use of your time. Perhaps some of these issues emerged from your management skills audit (see Appendix). As discussed in the case of Dominique, what support might be available to you to reduce some of the demands in each quadrant, for example, from the contracts or finance officer, team administrator, project workers and service users? Use the information from both exercises as a starting point for reprioritizing your workload and use of time. You could also replicate this exercise with team members in supervision and build up a picture of workload, what activities cause most stress to the team and what activities are likely to provide more satisfaction and contribute to the team's objectives.

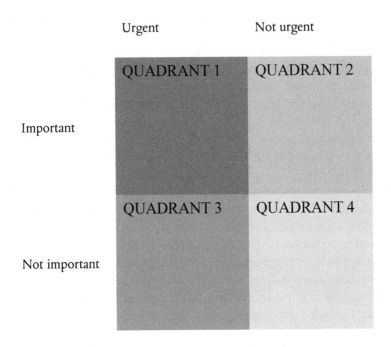

Figure 2.1: 'On the Spot' – The time management matrix
Source: adapted from Covey 2004

The above discussion highlights the bigger picture from which you can develop an awareness of the priorities or goals most valuable to you and your team. Allocating your time towards achieving these has to follow from achieving clarity about your routines and habits. Most time management programmes focus on individuals learning how to plan, attain and monitor different activities and at the end of this chapter we will conclude with some fundamental tips to keep these in check.

Procrastination

We all procrastinate at work, even when we are working under extreme pressure. Typical examples might include spending a lot of time complaining or feeling guilty about not having done something rather than just getting on with it. Repeatedly arriving unprepared for a meeting and then constantly apologizing for why we have not had time to start or complete a task is another common example. Van Eerde (2003) defined procrastination as typical avoidance behaviour, the avoidance of the execution of an intended action which is '(cognitively) important to the individual but is anticipated as something (affectively) unattractive' causing an 'approach-avoidance conflict' (p.422). In everyday terms, it results in an intrapersonal conflict between what you want to do and what you should do, and 'losing' it instead of solving it. Like us, you might recognize the distractions or displacement activities used to avoid emotional distress when one has something important to do, such as surfing the internet or rearranging the in-tray instead of getting on with what feels like an impending and unpleasant action. You would have recognized these activities represented in Covey's fourth quadrant in Figure 2.1. The inability to control one's attention and overcome barriers to using one's time effectively is at the core of procrastination (Van Eerde 2003). Whilst on the surface this appears to be dysfunctional behaviour, some have argued that the outcome of procrastination can cause such an acute pressure on time that this then presents us with a temporary challenge to achieve it. Being aware of your own tendencies for procrastination is the first step to dealing with why you might be doing it. Van Eerde (2003), having researched procrastination, argues for programmes which facilitate specific strategies to avoid it – for example, formal time management training. He asserts that time management is a learnable skill which allows people to experience greater structure and to obtain feelings of control.

Do it first every day

Forster (2006) has reframed the concept of procrastination in his concept of 'current initiative' which he describes as 'what you do first every day' (p.130). This is a regular focused action that keeps an initiative alive or keeps you engaged with it. Using Dominique as an example: Dominique needs to write her strategy document for the board of trustees which meets every three months. She knows this will take at least four hours. She carefully plans a half day in her diary about four weeks before the Board meeting is due. On that day, she comes into the office and there has been a flood in the staff toilets. This takes an hour to sort out and then she decides to just check her emails and meet with a member of staff before he goes off on leave. By midday she realizes that it is too late and looks in her diary for space to reschedule her report writing. She then realizes that she does not have a whole half day available until the week before the board.

Forster argues that doing activities little and often combined with 'doing it first' (p.131) will reduce opportunities for procrastination. If Dominique wrote a section of her report every week and did this first before anything else, even if it involved writing some headings, and then some notes under these headings, the daunting task of writing a report could feel easier. Forster argues that succeeding at something big involves giving yourself lots of opportunities for success along the way. Whatever your big initiative is, working on it every day or every week will aid progress and is more important than how long you work on it.

Technology and time management

Those in tune with IT and the latest technology will claim that the answer to time management lies in more sophisticated systems of handling information via electronic devices. There is no shortage of technological tools within social work and social care that can enhance workflow and enrich the knowledge base with which we work. However, the increasing use of ICT has also caused alienation in the social work and social care workforce. Munro (2010), for example, found that ICT systems are experienced as unhelpful in two ways: first, by requiring too much time for completing documentation and second, by spending insufficient time on the creation of service users' narratives, for example, chronologies for children which communicate their stories more meaningfully. Further, a lot of the data we collect – required for both national monitoring and local use – is said to be unhelpful in describing what is most important about our performance yet consumes a disproportionate amount of time and resources.

Email is probably one of the biggest drains on our time as it is possible to spend the entire working day engaged with email boxes and working through your inbox. Whilst this is a significant activity at work, it is, however, unlikely to have supported you in working towards your bigger objectives or enhanced the creative aspects of your work. Email is best tackled in short bursts in which incoming messages can be dealt with swiftly. Set aside time to do this, such as a half hour first thing in the morning; a sustained uninterrupted short specific period once or twice a day can help to avoid unproductive, time-consuming email flitting. Turn off the audio alert that sounds each time you receive a new email – which can be a distraction in itself. It is common practice to mark a read email as unread as a reminder that you need to deal with it. Approaching email as a continuous task amid other activities, however, is hugely inefficient. At first, keeping to these rules will take discipline. But over time discipline becomes habit.

Below are some key tips for setting up a simple and effective email reference system:

- Act decisively on messages so that they can be deleted or archived.

- Clear messages as effectively as possible.

- If a reply is required, send it. If some other action is required, such as reading an attachment, this can be done later. If the message may be needed at some point in the future, store it in a folder or create one for it.

- Make time to familiarize yourself with the tools associated with your email system such as macros, automatic messaging, search tools, reminders and calendars.

- Make a distinction between *reference information* and *action information*. *Reference information* is information that is not required to complete an action; it is information that you keep in case you need it later. Reference information is stored in your reference system – an email reference folder, in your documents folder or on the organizations intranet site.

  Action information is information you *must have* to complete an action. Action information is stored with the action. Most people receive a considerable amount of reference information through email, sometimes as much as one-third. Establish a system that makes it easy to transfer messages from your inbox into a series of email file folders where you store reference information to ensure you have easy access to it later.

If you are not technically competent, your time management can be adversely affected. Managers are beginning to engage far more with collaborative software such as wikis, bookmarking and social networking, which in the work environment can support people in both their individual and cooperative work particularly in being able to work virtually across the sector.

Technology as systems

As technology advances we will inevitably make more positive use of it within social work and social care and there are already a number of ongoing initiatives such as:

- Systems to help service users manage their own care through an e-marketplace by helping users to use the internet to purchase care, find information about services and assess their needs and plan their own support. This requires investment up-front in technology and training and can take some time before benefits are fully realized.

- Using predictive case models such as those being led by the Nuffield Trust to identify people who will require services or to score risk factors which can enable them to be monitored through virtual care environments where early or closer intervention can be developed. (Predictive case models use routinely collected electronic data to examine relationships between the factors present in an individual's situation in order to determine the expected future health care resource needed.)

- The potential of Telecare to save time by installing technology in the homes of service users to monitor and highlight needs for emergency support for those with long-term conditions.

- The use of multimedia advocacy where people with learning disabilities can use widely available technologies and software to create portfolios that explain their needs and engage them in decision making.

- Data capture via handheld PC tablets or digital pen technology which reduces the need for administrative support staff and automatically enters information into a central computer system as it is recorded; other touchscreen technologies offer mobile access to records increasing the potential for face to face contact with service users.

- Teleconferencing is developing a capacity to bring in specialist consultants and make use of robots and avatars so that staff can engage in virtual meetings saving travelling time.

- Virtual training and learning which make professional development more efficient as systems can also help to build records on professional and learning activities.

The use of technology needs to go hand in hand with the effective management of information and information literacy. Unethical use of information, for example, discourages information sharing and in turn reduces morale and discourages innovation.

According to Virkus (2003, p.1), to be information literate a person must be able to recognize when information is needed and have the ability to locate, evaluate and use effectively the needed information. This has been critiqued for its primary reliance on technological skills in themselves with less attention to the process of critical thinking. For example, information literacy has the potential for transforming our lifetime habits of using and evaluating information for personal, social and much wider purposes. Similarly, Shapiro and Hughes (1996) have argued that information literacy should not be restricted to 'functionally valuable technical skills' but should 'emphasise the importance of critical reflection on the nature of information itself, its technical infrastructure and its social, cultural and even philosophical context and impact' (p.31). Leading management theorists such as Drucker (1993) have emphasized the importance of preparing workers for the emerging knowledge society. One study found that professionals average 11 hours per week gathering information and 53 per cent of their time seeking out information (Bell 2002). Inability to utilize valuable information from the organization's information systems results in time wasted, and the inability to filter information may result in the wrong information being sent to service users, carers and other professionals. Within social care there has been a drive to encourage practitioners to engage with evidence and research to inform their practice. We know that access to knowledge is itself insufficient and that to be information literate people need to be able to:

- determine the nature and extent of the information needed

- access information effectively and efficiently

- evaluate information and its sources critically and incorporate selected information into their existing knowledge base and value system

- use information effectively to accomplish a specific purpose

- understand the economic, legal and social issues surrounding the access and use of information and use information ethically and legally

- engage in critical and contextual thinking about information in a knowledge economy and society.

Finally, technology is only helpful if it enhances what you are already doing. By and large, managers tend to be action orientated but they often find it difficult to spend time thinking about the way things are done in their organizations: this is relevant when we are told to use technology, which can then become a burden if it is not integrated into workflow and workload management appropriately.

Giving attention to 'workflow'

This final section touches on some barriers to developing a work management system. Research done by Delbridge, Gratton and Johnson (2006) into action-taking by managers identified three major traps that lock managers into non-action. The first relates to overwhelming demands where managers get caught in webs of expectations that completely overwhelm them. As illustrated in Dominique's situation, the demands on their everyday work leave little time for reflection or prioritization and, as a result, they lose sight of what really matters. Using Covey's tool to ensure you are busy on the right things can help you to develop an explicit personal agenda by reducing, prioritizing and organizing demands. Dominique will need to structure her contact time with staff and keep her eye on strategic demands by shaping and managing the expectations of her role. The second relates to the trap of unbearable constraints in social work and social care where over-bureaucratization and managerialist cultures make managers believe that they have little space for autonomous action. Focusing on these factors detracts from creativity. Delbridge et al. (2006) recommend mapping these constraints and thinking more systematically about how they can be overcome. Instead of lamenting limitations in general, purposeful managers identify with some precision the specific constraints that hinder their ability to achieve their goals. This may require tolerating conflict and ambiguity. Generating resources such as building a broader network of alliances in your organization and gaining access to non-material resources such as information, advice and expertise may be the pinch-point for your project. The third trap of non-action is unexplored choices. Being focused on the demands and constraints of their jobs, managers can develop tunnel vision and neglect their own personal development and sense of autonomy. After all, managers hold a lot of power. Purposeful managers are not only more aware of their choices but also consciously create choice by generating opportunities through conversations and interactions with others. Establishing clear goals, purposeful managers constantly explore the perspectives of others and generate new choices by involving them. This takes us back to the discussion at the beginning of the chapter about taking a more systemic approach to the organization and setting clear goals through collaboration.

Chapter summary

This chapter has given you some basic tools to start to manage your own time more effectively and through this the time of others. We have looked at issues in relation to both quantity and quality of time and at intrinsic and extrinsic factors impacting on our time management. Before reading the next chapter you are invited to go back to your time audit and ask yourself, how will you be able to create some space in your life? Asking this question is likely to require you to be tough on yourself. This may have been an issue that came up in your own management skills audit in relation to how your staff, colleagues and own manager perceive your availability or their relationships with you in your management role. Covey (2004) offered us some tips on how to create space which could help you to ring-fence some time for thinking or research and reflecting upon what you actually do. Your time audit and the exercise which identifies the key areas you are mostly engaged with may similarly generate ideas about which areas are open for swapping, stopping, doing or being more efficient. These may include issues to do with work–life balance such as we saw in Dominique's situation. If you never miss a meeting at work and feel you cannot let down work colleagues, why should you be expected to behave any differently with your own family, friends and loved ones? In Chapter 5 we will be looking at delegation as a skill for physically giving tasks to others to do on our behalf. This important management skill can also be useful in overcoming our own personal limitations and increases the number of goals or wider range of objectives we can accomplish simultaneously.

This brings us back to the issue of distributive leadership, as delegation involves a transfer of power and conferment of expertise to others. If done thoughtfully and supportively, delegation can be a dynamic tool for motivating and developing peers or team members to realize their full potential.

Action checklist

1. Create a supportive culture which facilitates communication.

2. Develop an awareness of the components of your workload management system and its strengths and areas for development.

3. Make time for creativity.

4. Achieve a balance in prioritizing demands on your time.

5. Acknowledge procrastination and turn it into a current initiative.

6. Engage and keep up with new technologies.

7. Stay focused on your goals and longer term objectives.

Chapter 3

Skills for Managing Change

Everything's Changed but What's Different?

*Everyone thinks of changing the world, but
no one thinks of changing himself.*
Leo Tolstoy

Introduction

Have you ever wondered if change at work would be so much easier if it were not for the people? There are many ways of seeing change, ranging from seeing it as an opportunity to a threat. Feelings will stretch from fear to excitement. Over time we might well experience a heady mixture, with personal temperament playing a part. Some of us look for change, others continuity. Your position in the organization will also be influential. The view of the organization from its headquarters' top floor strategy rooms is necessarily very different from that of the cook in one of its residential establishments. This chapter begins with an overview of some of the literature and research on change management. The chapter is underpinned by Smale's (1996) four levels of change management model and uses this model to take you through the different skills required to engage you in managing change.

> The new senior managers had thought about the current arrangements and had come to a clear view of how they needed to reorganize. They therefore set up some information and consultation sessions. The PowerPoint™ slides were impressive, with lots of colours and graphs and sounds. The invited audiences, drawn from across the organization, were, however, strangely silent. There were few questions and fewer comments.

> Several months later, the plans were looking ragged at the edges. There was new information about the area covered by the organization that had to be taken into account. Some of the proposed changes were in conflict with current employment policies, and widespread dissatisfaction had begun to come to the surface. Over coffee one day, the senior managers expressed bemusement: they had no idea how stuck in the past the workers and first-line managers were. The same day, two first-line managers met for lunch and expressed bemusement: how could senior management understand so little?

To help us look at this often messy process, we want to revisit Gerry and Rupa, two new managers whom we met in Chapter 1 of this book. Now in post for four months, they have a little more confidence in their abilities and a better sense of how things work in their teams. They have found mostly conscientious and committed people in their teams. Like nearly all new managers in their situation, they now believe that certain things can improve, and one or two need to improve. They have, however, experienced bigger changes such as that outlined at the start of this chapter, and are nervous about getting it wrong. Some changes had got stuck, and Gerry and Rupa had reservations about whether the changes actually worked. They want therefore to tackle changes in their team in a way that makes success more likely.

Gerry and Rupa will not lack advice from the literature; a search on www.amazon.co.uk using the keywords 'change management' in the spring of 2011 yielded 13,925 results. Most of this has taken the business world and organization-wide change as its main interest. Alimo-Metcalfe and Alban-Metcalfe (2006) have criticized much of the writing about change management for being gender biased and located mostly within the cultural context of America. Gerry and Rupa will need to approach change with these reservations in mind. They will find a heated debate about what constitutes appropriate leadership of change that mirrors the debate about leadership itself. In its review of the literature on leadership, the Performance and Innovation Unit, set up by the UK Labour Government, concluded that 'For practical people concerned about leadership, the theoretical literature can often be frustrating, obscure and contradictory' (2001, p.78).

Conventional approaches have drawn pictures of successful leaders of change as heroic, inspirational individuals, able to take thankful followers from darkness to light, and military metaphors are common. There is an increasing amount of research, however, that suggests that leadership is best seen as a product of relationships and as interactive in nature (Attwood *et al.* 2003). Some also argue that it is best seen as distributed throughout organizations. From this emerges the argument that successful change management is more about the skills of leaders in empowering, in working collaboratively and in supporting others in developing change management skills (Higgs and Rowland 2005, 2010). We will return to this later.

Gerry is concerned that his team's response to referrals about domestic violence is too limited. He has also been surprised that experienced workers in his team seem to look to him for decisions which he considers to be well within their abilities and responsibilities. Rupa sees her group of staff in the residential home as offering too much of a 'one size fits all' approach to care, and would also like to see progress on involving residents and carers more in the development of practice, and working on moving from a commitment to care to a more person-centred supportive approach. We turn to the literature to help us think about how they might move from these 'good ideas' to positive outcomes. We start with Gerry and Rupa as individuals.

Self-awareness and change

Our responses to change will vary along a continuum from needing change to feel alive to avoiding all but necessary changes. Across the life span, however, change is inevitable and our responses to it are what help shape us as people. In social work and social care, change is so pervasive that Rogers and Reynolds go as far as to assert that 'in health and social care services managing means managing change' (Rogers and Reynolds 2003, p.83). You are likely to find that you are managing several changes at once, from incremental (building on current practice) to transformational, which is a deeper level of change that will alter relationships in an organization and cause people to reflect on their values (Hafford-Letchfield 2009; Johnson and Williams 2007; Marris 1986).

Research by Higgs and Rowland (2010) found that those succeeding in bringing about change had high levels of self-awareness, a point supported by Binney *et al.* (2005, p.75) who argue that self-awareness enables leaders to be 'conscious of what drives them and their impact on others'. Gerry and Rupa need therefore to understand where they stand in relation to change both generally and specifically. They might find the summary in Chapter 1 of Hay's (2009) working styles' model useful, and some further suggestions about the impact of our preferred working styles on how we might set about managing change are summarized in Table 3.1.

Table 3.1: The impact of working styles on approaches to change

Working style	Pluses	Things to be aware of
Be perfect	Drawing up impeccable plans	Taking a long time over details
Be strong	Helping people feel safe when things are going wrong	Not acknowledging feelings aroused by change
Hurry up	Bringing energy and high work rate	Missing important details
Please people	Bringing empathy and commitment to collaboration	Expressing own views hesitantly
Try hard	Getting things going	Getting sidetracked by other interesting ideas

Source: based on Hay 2009

Knowing ourselves and our attitude to change helps us understand not just our own responses but also our impact on others, a key part of developing personal effectiveness in change management. Rupa, for example, might conclude that she has a tendency towards 'Please people'. This working style puts others' needs before your own, and she will need to be careful therefore not to compromise just to please others as she sets about establishing a more individualized approach to support. She will, however, find that this style helps her with engaging with others, one of the key skills in bringing about change. If Gerry, on the other hand, finds some of the 'Be perfect' in his approach to change, he needs to be mindful of the need to dot every 'i' and cross every 't', because this will risk slowing the process down unnecessarily. His preferred style will, however, help him to spot the important 'smaller print' aspects of change that others might miss and which become significant later on. For both, the ability to understand themselves is essential if they are to set about attempting to improve practice through others.

What do we know about change management initiatives?

Skills in self-awareness provide the first building block for any manager wanting to bring about change. We want to add to this some thoughts on the process itself, on what might make success more likely. Such analysis helps clarify the skills needed for change management.

Gerry and Rupa are right to be cautious as they seek to improve practice because the research evidence about change is not reassuring. Miller (2002, p.360), for example, states that 'most independent research shows change failure rates running at about 70 per cent', and others, for example, Armenakis and Harris (2009) and Higgs and Rowland (2005, 2010) make the same point. In social work, messages from public inquiries into serious incidents have also alerted us to the problems that reorganizations can cause (Jones 2001). Reflecting on one UK serious case review of the death of a child at risk, Peter Connolly, Jones wrote that front line workers 'will again experience the chaos of organizational change, with even more time spent keeping records and responding to inspectors. Their managers will be distracted by producing more strategies and reports' (Jones 2008).

Doyle, Claydon and Buchanan's research (2000) revealed a very mixed picture of change, with a number of negative outcomes reported. Among these were damage to working relationships, damage to people, deterioration in worker commitment, loss of important knowledge and experience, and an increase in burnout. Such outcomes would be very concerning in organizations where worker commitment and motivation are closely connected to service quality. In a situation similar to Rupa's, where an organization wanted to bring about a more individualized approach to residential care, Conklin (2010) found that the approach taken by management had caused the process to stall, almost stop, even though direct care staff were in agreement with overall aims. Conklin concluded that 'to succeed the change agent must find a way of joining the conversation that is unfolding, rather than simply drowning it out with the announcement that something new and better has arrived' (2010, p.490).

Trying to get it right

No one sets out to fail at change and, viewed from a distance, all attempts at change in organizations look much the same:

- An idea develops somewhere that some things are not working as well as they might.

- An individual or group of people then work on bringing about the changes thought to be necessary.

- The change gets implemented – or not.

Sometimes (though not always) there will also be evidence of review and evaluation. This typical chronology of change means that many of the most widely read and quoted books on change refer to a framework which describes 'stages' of change (Cameron and Green 2009; Kotter 1996; Lewin 1951). These writers agree that success is associated with good communication skills and stakeholder involvement. As we move closer to particular changes, however, many differences become apparent in approaches to communication and involvement. Linked to this is the debate about the nature of leadership in change.

There's no guarantee of success, but...

It would be a foolhardy manager who embarked on trying to bring about change thinking that success was guaranteed. It is true, however, that some ways of approaching it appear more likely to lead to a successful outcome than others. The starting point for this is the way that people leading change understand the nature of leadership. We referred earlier to the hot debate about this in the literature. Increasingly in recent years researchers have been arguing against the idea of change needing charismatic, inspirational leaders. Research by Higgs and Rowland (2005, 2010) found that such people – 'movers and shakers' who set the pace for change and set out to persuade and cajole – are actually associated with *failure*. Binney *et al.* (2005) reported similar findings from their action research. They found that leaders who 'knew the answer' and did 'to others' achieved 'compliance'. Binney *et al.* referred to these as 'people paying lip service to the new ways of thinking and behaving, but not the change in hearts and minds that they sought' (2005, pp.196–7). On the other hand, those who succeeded made themselves part of the process, engaging and listening to others, and developing their ideas as others developed theirs. They displayed skills of engagement and empathy, and were willing to tolerate the uncertainty that working with others' perspectives will bring. Higgs and Rowland (2005, 2010, 2011) found that successful leaders are skilful at:

- 'framing change' – working with others to develop vision and give others space to make change happen

- 'creating capacity' – helping others develop change management skills, giving feedback and coaching

- ensuring that people work across boundaries to effect the change.

This set of findings sits comfortably with the idea of 'distributed leadership', an approach which recognizes that leadership roles can be taken by many more than just official leaders (see, for example, Alimo-Metcalfe and Alban-Metcalfe 2006). Box 3.1 gives examples of two potential different styles in relation to the communication and involvement required from followers.

There are, then, important questions for Rupa and Gerry to ask as they begin to work on their ideas for improvement. How will I work with my team on this? How much of their involvement will I allow? This takes us back to the importance of communication and involvement. Depending on the model of leadership that they adopt, these will have different purposes. Box 3.1 shows the extremes of this.

If Rupa chooses to 'announce' her decision about changing to a more individualized model of care, as Leader A would, she risks achieving compliance rather than commitment. She also risks leaving unsaid the many ideas that carers will have about making it happen better. B's style is empowering, a style endorsed by research in care settings by Boehm and Yoels (2008) and by Chalfont and Hafford-Letchfield (2010). Both sets of authors found empowerment to be associated with success in achieving changes in practice.

This newer view of leadership as collaborative and relationship-based rather than dictatorial and distant is a challenge to many of the more established approaches, and perhaps reflects changes in wider society. How might Gerry and Rupa move, though, from a commitment to engaging others to achieving the changes that they see as important? To explore this, and the skills that they will need, we will make use of the work of Smale and his colleagues at the former National Institute for Social Work (Smale 1996, 1998; Smale, Tuson and Statham 2000). This was developed from collaboration and research on change with health care and social work and social care organizations.

Box 3.1: Communication and involvement in change – A means to an end!

Leader A: wanting to drive change from above
Communicates to get the message across. Talks more than listens. Sees 'resistance' as a barrier to overcome. Keeps communication at the cognitive level. Likely to see expressions of concern as 'whinging'.

Involves people as a means to gain their agreement. Behaves as though the organization is a machine.

Leader B: wanting to engage with others to achieve change
Communicates to understand others' perspectives. Listens more than talks. Sees resistance as information about the change or his/her behaviour in relation to it. Is able to engage with emotions, including negative ones.

Involves people as a means of understanding better the value of change, and as a means of developing ideas collectively. Behaves as though organization is made up of people.

Moving from thinking into action

Understanding ourselves and establishing our style in leading change provide a strong base for developing personal effectiveness. We noted earlier that many texts on change adopt a 'stages' approach (Cameron and Green 2009; Kotter 1996; Lewin 1951). These models are helpful in providing an overall framework, but care is needed in applying a linear model that suggests neatness in a world which is often messy and volatile. Smale (1996, p.97) prefers to think in terms of interlinking levels and identifies four levels.

- *Level 1*: Asking, what needs to change? And what needs to stay the same?

- *Level 2*: Undertaking an analysis of what Smale terms the 'innovation trilogy':
  - key individuals
  - the change, to inform action planning
  - the context in which the change will happen.
- *Level 3*: Starting negotiations, and ensuring that the focus remains on organizational and staff development issues.
- *Level 4*: Paying attention to evaluation through obtaining and using feedback to inform further planning.

Smale (1996) also argues that we need to unpack our assumptions about change. He makes the important point that our approach to change will be influenced by a set of assumptions. Look at his assumptions in Table 3.2, and use these to prompt your own thoughts. The second column gives you room for notes. How do these assumptions influence how you then set about responding to or initiating change?

We will now go on to consider how Smale's levels might be useful to consider how Gerry and Rupa set about achieving the changes that they see as necessary. To recap:

- Gerry would like to see a better response to reports of domestic violence, along with workers being willing and able to take more responsibility for decision making.

- Rupa would like a more individualized approach to care, and more involvement from residents and carers in the development of the service.

In thinking about these, Gerry and Rupa realize that the changes that they seek are connected. Gerry sees that a focus on change to domestic violence referrals will help develop a culture of individuals taking more responsibility, as long as he allows people a genuine voice or stake in the service. Rupa links individualized care with the need to achieve greater user involvement. She realizes that she cannot achieve this without also empowering front line staff. Both therefore make an important link between their leadership style and their approach to change.

Table 3.2: 'On the Spot' – Comparing assumptions about change

Smale's assumptions	How relevant or true are they for me?
Change and continuity always go together.	
Change needs managing (no matter how good the ideas are).	
Change needs the commitment of front line workers.	
Change initiatives are best seen as attempts to solve problems.	
The 'machine' metaphor for organizations is rarely helpful.	
We should not assume that all change is good change, and so feedback on its impact is critical.	
We should judge the results of change initiatives by their consequences, not by whether the change happens or not.	
Change needs to be seen as an ongoing aspect of any well-functioning team or organization.	

Level 1: Change and continuity

A number of authors have noted that there is a danger when attempting to manage change that we focus only on making the change itself (Binney *et al.* 2005; Birkinshaw and Gibson 2005; Cameron and Green 2009; Graetz and Smith 2010). Change and continuity coexist and therefore need balancing. Graetz and Smith (2010, p.136) remind us that 'change is a natural phenomenon which is intimately entwined with continuity'. Perhaps for Gerry and Rupa the questions are straightforward:

- What do I think needs to change?

- What should stay the same?

Addressing these questions helps to establish a clear initial focus for discussion, and responds to what many of us seek in entering periods of change: a reassurance that some, perhaps most, aspects of our lives will remain the same. Attwood *et al.* (2003) make an important contribution here with their idea of 'holding frameworks'. They argue that leaders need to communicate 'the core purpose, desired identity and values of the organization' (p.37). Attention to these, they argue, enables shared understandings to emerge that 'can become fixed points in a sea of change' (p.37). Research by Burnes and Jackson (2011) emphasized the importance of aligning the values underpinning change with individual and organizational values. In social work and social care settings, this relationship between individual and organizational values and the intended change is crucial, given that organizational effectiveness depends so much on individual behaviour.

Level 2: The 'innovation trinity'

The next level, with its three linked elements, is really the heart of this approach, and requires skills in analysis. In order to do this successfully managers need the ability to stand back from the situation and try to gain an objective view. Level 2 helps with this.

Element 1: Identifying the key people

We noted earlier how differing leadership approaches can influence how we involve others: at one extreme change leaders sit above the process, at the other they see themselves as part of the process. Smale's ideas fit into the latter category. Key people need to be identified not as a precursor to working out how to persuade them about change, but in order to begin discussions with them. In particular, he produces strong arguments about the value of seeking 'convergence', a coming together of ideas, which might well start with identifying the opposite – divergence. This might not be about whether change is needed (there might well be convergence over this) but about what form change might take. As Routledge and Sanderson (2000) note in writing about the introduction of person-centred planning in Oldham, this might be counter to what many organizations feel comfortable with, exposing them as it might to what they dismiss as 'whinging'.

There are however a number of reasons for taking this approach:

- Not being willing to hear views heightens the risk of failure because people do not feel ownership. The opposite also holds:

the more that people have had a voice in planning change, the more committed they usually are to its success.

- It is possible that a proposal for change is misguided, so that dissenting voices offer an important contribution (Armenakis and Harris 2009; Ford, Ford and Amelio 2008).

- Change provokes a wide range of feelings in those subject to it (Attwood *et al.* 2003; Duck 1993; Furze and Gale 1996; Graetz and Smith 2010; Kotter and Cohen 2002). Marris, a sociologist, argued that this can amount to a process similar to bereavement (Marris 1986). This will not be the case with all change, but the loss cycle is worth bearing in mind when we look at responses to change as illustrated in Figure 3.1.

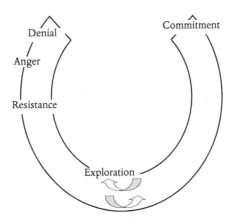

Figure 3.1: The loss cycle in organizational change

The influence of power is crucial. Marris asserts that:

> Reformers have already assimilated these changes to their purpose and worked out a reformulation which makes sense to them, perhaps through months or years of analysis or debate. If they deny others the chance to do the same, they treat them as puppets dangling by the threads of their own conceptions. (Marris 1986, p.155)

Gerry has spent time thinking about possible changes: now he needs to give his team the space to do the same. In his time with the team trust will have developed, such that he might find a receptive group willing to think about improvements to their practice. Smale argues that people will occupy a variety of positions in relation to change. Some by temperament are likely to be early adopters, some more cautious. Given that change often 'needs legs' to be effective, it is helpful to have early adopters around, though equally important are 'opinion leaders' (people with personal influence) who might become 'product champions', who see the positive benefits of the change. This mapping of key people needs some thought, to avoid missing people who are important but less visible. These might be people outside the organization – service users, other agencies and so on – or people in different parts of the same organization. In the person-centred changes in Oldham for example, Routledge and Sanderson (2000) identified service users and colleagues in Human Resources, finance and training as key people. Therefore the sorts of questions you might want to consider are:

- Who sees what as a problem?

- Who is likely to be supportive?

- Who might oppose it?

- Who might gain from it?

- Who might lose?

- How can we give time to people who are facing loss?

Rupa will be aware of the different personalities in her team. She might, for example, suspect that some people will oppose the change to more individualized care because they have become used to the way of working over many years. Opening up debate through team meetings and supervision, however, might lead to surprises for her. She might find people are more keen on changes than she realizes.

Element 2: The nature of the change

Change comes in all shapes and sizes (Hafford-Letchfield 2009; Johnson and Williams 2007; Marris 1986), from incremental to transformational. Smale therefore counsels against 'one size fits all'. Some changes are easily adoptable, because they strike a chord with those needing to implement them, are consistent with values, are fairly simple and their impact can be easily seen. Others are the opposite. Questions for you to consider here are:

- How adoptable is it?

- Has it happened successfully elsewhere?

- Would a trial help?

If this analysis demonstrates that the proposed change looks as though it might be difficult, this is not a reason to abandon it. Some of the greatest reforms (think of slavery, the vote for women) have faced enormous opposition. However, undertaking a more detailed analysis helps to identify obstacles more clearly. In recent years we have seen the opposite in practice where central government has made rapid leaps from 'pilots' to full implementation, which leave little or no time for evaluation and learning (Preston-Shoot 2009).

Element 3: The context for the change

Change will occur in many different contexts. The same change will prove more difficult in some places than others. All teams, for example, will have their own power dynamics and history, such that some will be more receptive than others. For some people, change fatigue will mean that one more change is one change too many.

Some of the questions about context therefore are:

- What else is happening?

- Does the change fit the culture or challenge it?

- Will the change be vulnerable to people's sense of change fatigue?

Gerry and Rupa will not know the attitudes of their teams without further discussion. These might demonstrate a variety of positions. From our experience, this variety might not come out clearly through team discussions, where powerful voices might dominate. A study into transactions within supervision (Bourn and Hafford-Letchfield 2011) offers further insight into the strategies used by managers to enhance relationships with front line staff, and provides pointers to the skills required by managers who often have to trade between the needs of supervisees and the organization in order to support and develop effective and quality practice.

Bringing the three elements together

These three elements make up what Smale calls the 'trinity' of managing change. The reason why this exercise in analysing any proposed change is so important is contained in the often quoted 'Failing to plan is planning to fail'. Sound planning sets the agenda for moving into action.

Level 3: Implementation

Our earlier analysis should have mapped what needs discussing with whom: so that negotiation skills (our focus in Chapter 7) now move to centre stage. Here we want to note that action requires high-level interpersonal skills. This includes skilful negotiation concerning:

- the extent to which those who will make the change happen have the necessary skills and knowledge

- how to respond to those who will experience a sense of loss in the process

- how the success of the change will be evaluated, and by whom

- what resources are needed, and whether these will be new resources or a reusing of existing ones.

It is clear from the literature that changes will need different levels and kinds of attention. A change to a new software system because of upgrading, for example, might well need some training for those using it, but is unlikely to impact on their values. With Gerry's wish for change in the team's response to domestic violence, he might find general support but questions about resources. He will need in his analysis of key people to consider views beyond his team. For example, what are the perspectives of people who have had contact with his team because of domestic violence? In seeking more user involvement in the development of the service, Rupa will also need to look beyond the immediate environment, perhaps to more senior management and local user groups. She would be well advised to look at national evidence: Beresford *et al.*'s (2011) research would, for example, provide her with powerful material about both the research on user involvement and the change process. All of this reinforces Smale's point that change rarely follows a neat linear process. Instead, managers find their attention going back and forth across levels.

Level 4: Feedback and evaluation

Evaluation is a process which involves looking back systematically at what has been accomplished and measuring the present position against its original aims (Coleman and Earley 2005). As a management activity, evaluation is an integral part of the change management cycle and takes us back to one of Smale's assumptions: that change should be judged not by whether it happens or not but by its impact. It is all too easy to become competitive with anyone who opposes the change, creating a 'win–lose' contest in which bringing about the change becomes more important than the results of the change. The purpose of evaluation is not to prove, but to *im*prove and provides a formal process of judging the 'value' of something, for example, the assessment of the effects and effectiveness of an innovation, intervention, policy, practice or service (Byford and Sefton 2003). It is usually focused on outcomes, which are the changes, benefits or other effects that happen as a result of an organization's activities (Hafford-Letchfield 2010). Glendinning *et al.* (2008) define different clusters of desired outcomes: first, change outcomes which enable you to measure the output or impact of change on something or someone; and, second, what they call process outcomes, which refer to the experience of the change itself, for example, staff feeling respected, or service users having a say. Box 3.2 provides an example of evaluating change with an outcome focus, evaluating the extent which the change has achieved what was hoped for.

> **Box 3.2: Questions for evaluating person-centred planning**
>
> - How well are people empowered in the planning process?
> - How good are the plans (for example, including how well they reflect what is important to the person, in the actions being allocated to people with dates for achieving them)?
> - Are goals being achieved and people's lives changing as a result?

Giving attention to impact relates closely to another reason for investing time in evaluation: change gives rise to learning, but only if time is taken to capture it. This learning has two aspects:

- First, it can lead to changes in emphasis or direction before it is too late (Binney *et al.* 2005; Pfeffer and Sutton 2006).

- Second, learning feeds into future activities to bring about change (Horwath and Morrison 2000).

Pfeffer and Sutton (2006) argue that whether learning is possible needs to be part of the planning from the start. If any plan to change does not have the opportunity for learning, they argue, or if the organization is not good at learning, then the change project will be a higher risk. Binney *et al.* (2005) come at learning from a slightly different angle, as something which must engage all involved in change: 'in a transition the leader must see herself and the others as part of a collective process of learning' (p.197). This conscious commitment to reviewing the impact of change can also, as Horwath and Morrison (2000) point out, produce evidence of things working – and therefore reason to celebrate success. Not that the impact of change can be evaluated in a once and for all way. Gerry and Rupa might find that small changes over time add up to something substantial, and they will need to able to celebrate small successes along the way.

Chapter summary

In this chapter we have established that there is no guarantee that an attempt to lead change will be successful. However, with a review of the literature and through the case studies, we have tried to demonstrate that skilful and thoughtful approaches by people willing not only to lead but to listen, engage and collaborate with others is more likely to succeed when leading change. This may well be a more demanding style for busy managers, and it becomes vital that people in Gerry and Rupa's position establish and maintain their own strong support networks. The effort should be worth it, however. Through it, change becomes a partner in the continuing quest for improvements in service, not an unwelcome intruder on the status quo.

Action checklist

1. Be aware of your own attitudes and beliefs about change as these can affect the culture in which changes are introduced.

2. Skills in participation, consultation and active listening and responding to people's concerns are the most valuable skills required by managers.

3. Evaluate and learn from your own and others' experiences of change.

Chapter 4

Recruiting and Selection

Getting the Right Colleagues and Striving Towards Happiness

A round man cannot be expected to fit in a square hole
straight away. He must have time to modify his shape.
Mark Twain

Introduction

Recruitment and selection of colleagues is an area of competence for all
managers. Much of the literature on workforce development in social
work and social care bypasses discussion of the actual skills required.
Building on the guidelines available in the sector, this chapter explores
the initial actions and considerations when planning staff recruitment
and the process of selecting an individual from a pool of applicants.
Incorrect assumptions about class, gender, sexual orientation, ethnic
group, culture, religion age or physical ability, and indeed any other
type of discrimination, can affect objectivity in recruitment and
selection and contravene legislation that protects individuals from
discrimination. It is important to consider these influences at every
step of the process, including how other more subtle prejudices may
be generated by particular organizational traditions regarding the 'type
of person' considered suitable for a particular role. The qualities of the
successful applicant should match what the organization requires but
good recruitment practice enables you to identify people who facilitate
flexibility in their practice. Recruitment and selection is integral to
service development and its ability to respond to evolving users' needs
and other demands in relation to emerging policy and legislation.

It is not difficult to discriminate in the recruitment and selection
process through personal responses and reactions to certain types of

people or by succumbing to the pressure to fill a gap which is currently causing stress within your service. The consequences of not recruiting the right person to the job cannot be underestimated, not only because of the high costs associated with the recruitment process but its ongoing impact on the quality of the service and team morale.

This chapter will consider how the assessment methods used during the recruitment and selection process can be as fair and transparent as possible, by linking each stage to any specific requirements of employment legislation and practice guidance. We will start by considering some generic issues documented by research on the social care workforce. This provides the strategic context for our recruitment and selection activities and informs management responsibilities that go beyond this initial stage of workforce planning. Building on a case study, we then go on to look at some practical skills required for effective practice in recruitment and selection, giving examples of how to write job descriptions and person specifications, and then how to devise clear criteria and assessment techniques to assess applicants' competence and potential. The case study will serve to illustrate these different stages and identify the skills required for engaging in the process.

Key issues in workforce planning

The challenges for social care and some of its partner agencies are ongoing, supported by a growing body of research evidence:

> Bringing commissioning, financial and workforce strategies into balance is no easy job. The workforce is so often a minor consideration, yet it is an essential ingredient in the mix. The results of this survey are beginning to highlight the gaps and successes particularly with integrated workforce strategies. (Mun Thong Phung Director, London Borough of Haringey, cited in Skills for Care 2009, p.x)

Despite intense media criticism, social work has never been more relevant to the challenges of contemporary society, and remains a popular choice of degree and career. Through the National Minimum Data Set for Social Care (NMDS-SC) (Skills for Care 2010b) quantitative information is captured regularly alongside qualitative studies conducted through bodies such as the Social Care Workforce Research Unit. Both sources provide us with a rich evidence base about the social work and social care workforce in the UK and intelligence for future planning. We know that services are delivered by a large, diverse and dispersed workforce. Social care is now one of the largest workforces in the UK within which people are individually employed or may work in small businesses as well as very large corporations. We have summarized a few of the challenges and opportunities that impact on any workforce development strategy in Box 4.1, which is just a summary of the rich research beginning to emerge about our sector. Given the increasing impact of globalization and austerity on human resources in public services, it is even more imperative to ensure that people are treated properly, even when tough management decisions which affect their current and future employment are being taken (Prosser 2010).

The research evidence also illustrates that good recruitment, selection and retention practice would appear to be a moral issue. Good practice is essential to both short- and long-term aims, and can benefit the reputation and the overall health of the sector. Skilful practice in this area is not just concerned with mindful, fair and transparent recruitment, but has to incorporate retention strategies through staff care and work–life balance. Strategies might include the provision of quality supervision, appraisal, flexibility, career progression, training and qualifications, team building and the right to enjoy safe and harmonious relationships at work.

The recruitment process

The remainder of this chapter outlines the steps required to select and recruit staff and will build on the case study below where appropriate for illustration.

> Naresh is a service manager for a Local Authority Children and Young People's Service. The service has been substantially restructured to include an 'Initial Response Team' which screens all new contacts and makes a judgement about whether they meet the criteria for a service from Children's Social Care. Naresh has been working across a number of key agencies to develop threshold criteria agreed at a strategic level. The service is now supported by a range of intensive prevention and other services alongside brokerage to ensure social workers remain focused on those families experiencing complex issues and risk. The initial response team comprises very experienced and skilled staff from multidisciplinary backgrounds who are

supervised by a consultant social worker. Naresh still needs to recruit the consultant social worker, a new post for an experienced person who wishes to retain practice expertise combined with some management responsibilities. Besides managing the above team, this person needs to ensure that all referrals not judged to require an intervention from Children's Social Care are signposted or referred on appropriately. They also need to offer consultation and advice to other professionals on safeguarding issues; provide training and on-going liaison with other agencies; track patterns of referrals and contacts by type and by agency; and to investigate and help support and stabilize accepted referrals from children and families in crisis in their first week of contact. The role is completely new and Naresh knows that the person appointed is absolutely crucial to making the new service a success.

Box 4.1: Summary of research findings on the social care workforce

- Opportunities to obtain qualifications and their impact on career pathways are recognized factors in retaining staff in the care sector (Nakhnikian and Kahn 2004).

- Good recruitment and retention of staff make a direct, relevant and substantial contribution to front line performance.

- For commissioners, managing staff shortages is a key quality indicator. Ensuring contracts with care providers are adequately financed for appropriate staffing promotes better safeguarding practice.

- Workforce planning includes having an understanding and knowledge with local partners in relation to provision.

- Rising numbers of people using social care services are becoming employers themselves adding to the complexity of workforce relationships. This will increase as individualization of care progresses.

- Debates about costs, quality and the reality of enhanced user choices are leading towards greater outsourcing of staff employment, particularly in adult care (Improvement and Development Agency 2008).

- A detailed profile of international social care workers (Hussein, Stevens and Manthorpe 2010) demonstrates the vital role played in those vacancies difficult to fill and offer positive and enriching experiences within the care sector.

- Overseas recruits tend to experience more racism, bullying and discrimination, particularly from service users and carers.

- Research with refugees shows that medical, education and welfare professionals struggle to utilize their skills because of an expensive and time-consuming conversion system, yet have much to offer from perspectives that can help institutions cater for the needs of new communities and the personalization agenda (HM Government 2007).

- Within adult social care, most of the older and younger workers are recruited to adult residential services, such as care homes. Older workers are over-represented in adult day care and community care.

- Younger people are more likely to be female, travel shorter distances to work, but less likely to be from Black and minority ethnic groups. Nearly half were recruited from outside the sector highlighting the importance of designing wider recruitment campaigns so as to attract young people to the care sector.

- Research revealed blinkered perspectives of men towards careers in social care requiring targeting of key age groups (20–25 and 50+) particularly in some rural areas (Skills for Care 2010a). Using promotional packages linked to redundancy may increase male entrants to different parts of the sector.

- Trends in the workforce continue to reflect marginalization of some groups. For example, men still dominate senior management; women are more likely to be working in the front line and in the lowest paid caring roles. Succession planning remains a barrier for Black and minority staff (Manthorpe *et al.* 2010).

- Intellectual capital is vital within discussions about retention (Prosser 2010). Organizations need to capitalize on knowledge – their most valuable asset – held by their members through their contacts, networks, skills, knowledge and experience.

However, few organizations in social work and social care have time or resources to make a systematic attempt to assess their 'human capital' and appraise how well it is used.

- Cornes *et al.* (2010b) found agency workers playing an important role in 'keeping the show on the road' (p.10). Agency workers were able to get through high volumes of work and refresh teams by bringing in new skills and insights from other areas.

- Advantages for agency workers themselves include flexibility and opportunities for broadening practice experiences, especially for newly qualified social workers, and gaining the experience and insight needed to find and secure the right permanent job.

- Imbalances between permanent and temporary staff in teams are likely to be more symptomatic of underlying organizational issues, and can contribute towards poor safeguarding practice. This is attributed to lack of continuity, commitment or investment in their induction, supervision and training (Cornes *et al.* 2010b).

- Agency working can be a means of escaping deteriorating conditions of employment and relational issues can often affect people's reasons for seeking alternative employment. These types of issues are often overlooked in recruitment and retention strategies but need to be tackled.

- Using equality audit tools facilitates equality in workforce planning. The Workplace Equality Index (WEI), for example, allows organizations to benchmark their performance in terms of equality for lesbian, gay and bisexual staff. It helps organizations to assess what they need to do to improve their workplace for lesbian, gay and bisexual staff and to consider what impact this will have on the organization more broadly (Stonewall 2010).

Drafting job descriptions and person specifications

Recruitment involves working through a series of stages including defining the role clearly, attracting applicants, managing the overall application and selection process and making the appointment. Scott, Gill and Crowhurst (2008, p.110) identify two main organizational approaches to recruitment:

1. *Job centred*: The essential activities of the job, the expertise and the person characteristics are defined and the advertisement is placed. This is the right approach for Naresh in relation to his new team above.

2. *Placement approach*: Staff suitable to join the organization are recruited and then trained for certain roles. This approach is commonly used in 'Grow Your Own' initiatives for social work (Noble, Harris and Manthorpe 2009) or in graduate schemes where people are encouraged to take on a bespoke training course so that their roles are tailored to specific organizational needs. This approach is specifically used to target service development needs and succession planning.

INVOLVING SERVICE USERS AND CARERS

More organizations are beginning to involve service users and carers in selection and recruitment, and service users themselves have highlighted this issue as crucial if they are to be fully involved in planning and delivering services. This requires attention to planning, training and resourcing the process. Factors found to promote effective user involvement include: commitment from staff and service users; good support, liaison and collaboration with trade unions and personnel departments; networking; and involving people throughout the process. Barriers to involvement may include employers' scepticism that service users are unable to maintain confidentiality, or to work within equal opportunities guidelines. Research has showed, however, that with training, practice, and careful and adequate support, most people were able to participate successfully and provide valuable information about applicants' attitudes towards working with service users. Service users can be involved in all stages of the process, and should be in order to avoid tokenism.

Stage 1: Job analysis

Before recruiting for a new or existing position it is important to invest time in gathering information about the nature of the job. This means thinking not only about the content and the tasks making up the job, but also the job's purpose, the outcomes expected from the post holder and how these fit with the organization's structure, responsibilities and objectives. This analysis forms the basis of a job description (JD) and person specification (PS). Job descriptions are necessary to define responsibilities and accountabilities and are important in helping employees to have a clear understanding of what their roles mean in practice. A job description should define the post as clearly as possible and enable objectives to be set for the member of staff recruited. A good job description can also be used in supervision and appraisal as it forms the basis of the contract of employment. For most roles in social work and social care, the use of National Occupational Standards (NOS) is essential as they describe best practice by bringing together skills, knowledge and values. Naresh will need to utilize the Professional Capabilities Framework for Social Workers (see Figure 4.1) which in England provides an overarching set of nine core standards for social workers. These encompass competence and conduct, and are a particularly useful reference to inform the drafting of a PS and the *level* of competence required for each standard. Naresh would, for example, give consideration to these levels of competency, given that his post holder will have supervisory and management responsibilities.

For other job descriptions, managers using NOS may find that these help to reinforce the link between strategy and operational management. Job descriptions should also be aligned with service standards. NOS offer a common language for achieving this sort of relationship (Skills for Care 2006). Whilst initially NOS were used as the basis for qualifications in social care, wider uses are now emerging, for example, within human resource management.

Stage 2: Write a job description

1. Think carefully about the job itself and what is special or specific about it. Will the job form part of a more generic role in your organization or merit a more tailored JD? For example, the post of consultant social worker is quite a specific post but Naresh will want to keep in mind any flexibility required as the role and service develops.

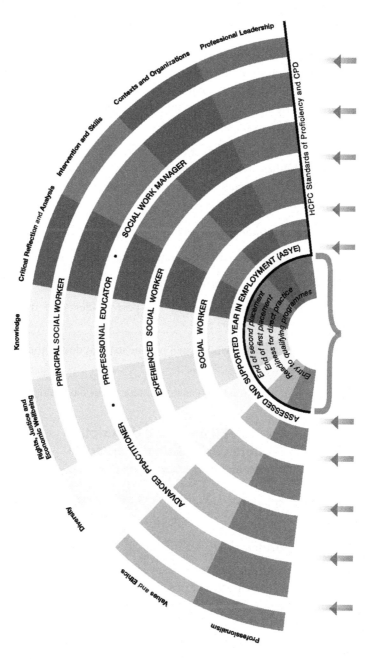

Figure 4.1: Professional Capabilities Framework for Social Workers

2. Identify the different tasks the person is expected to do and group these together. Remember to refer to any other relevant standards. In the example JD given in Box 4.2, these tasks have been grouped in relation to three areas: the service, the team and the service users. Most of the key capabilities for social work, such as 'Professional Leadership', 'Knowledge' and 'Values and Ethics' (see Figure 4.1), will need to be evidenced. This will be achieved by spelling out in the accompanying PS the criteria being used to assess such evidence.

3. Write a single statement which covers the postholder's main responsibilities. The job purpose/summary in Box 4.2 attempts to provide an overall description of what the post holder is expected to do.

Generally a job description should have five clear areas:

1. Job title, which should be accurate, relevant, clear and creative.

2. Job purpose, stated clearly and attractively.

3. Reporting mechanisms, telling the post holder who they are accountable and report to.

4. Key accountabilities which spell out the explicit duties, their scale and extent.

5. Terms and conditions such as hours, salary, holidays and training.

Box 4.2: Example job description – Consultant Social Worker

Job location: London Borough of Flava

Job title: Consultant Social Worker

Reports to: Service Manager Children and Young People's Service

Responsible for: Initial Response Team

Job purpose/summary: To manage all aspects of the Initial Response Team's activity, to a high standard and in accordance with the Children Act 1989, 2004 and associated policy and practice guidance. Provide professional consultation and training to a range of professionals and partner agencies on safeguarding issues and take a lead in developing and implementing safeguarding policies

---

and procedures including main responsibility for performance management of activity in relation to initial assessments and pathways of families using the initial response service.

Duties and responsibilities

The service

- Contribute to the vision and strategy of the Children and Young People's service and provide leadership to the team.

- Prepare, implement and review the business plan of the Initial Response Team and contribute to other service plans where appropriate.

- Collaborate and develop strategic and operational networks with other professional groups and services in relation to the development of the service.

- Assess and develop a training plan for staff from the Children and Young People's Service that helps them to meet the aims and objectives of the service.

- Ensure high standards of assessment, care and support are provided and maintained within current legislation and the organization's policies.

- Manage the team's recruitment and retention strategy and contribute to those of other teams in the service.

- Manage the team budget; provide timely and accurate financial information and other resources according to the organization's directives.

- Maintain up-to-date and accurate records as required for the effective and efficient running of the team as may be required by the service performance management system.

- Ensure the health, safety and welfare of individuals who use services and staff by implementing and abiding by the relative legislation and requirements.

- Ensure the safe, proper use of technology within the team.

- Design, develop and use effective and appropriate quality monitoring systems in order to assess the performance of the team and the service with regard to its aims and objectives.

- Provide regular management reports as required and design, implement and evaluate an information and advice strategy.

Staff

- Ensure that recruitment and employment policies and procedures are current and applied fairly and consistently.

- Design, implement and supervise staff work rotas to ensure that adequate cover is provided, and that the workload is delegated appropriately, and meets the legislative and policy requirements of the service and the needs of children and families.

- Provide management cover and cover for other teams within the Children and Young People's service, according to an established rota.

- Ensure that information about staff is handled confidentially and in accordance with Data Protection legislation.

- Develop and implement staff development, supervision, training and appraisal programmes so that staff are supported, and competent to perform the full range of duties allocated to them.

- Establish and ensure regular team meetings and attend and organize meetings with other management, staff and professional groups as required to develop and maintain good working relationships within the service.

- Design, implement and evaluate training programmes for uni-professional and multi-professional groups on skills, knowledge and competencies in relation to the service needs.

- Maintain and enhance harmonious relationships between those people you work with considering, in particular, the well-being of staff in the team.

People who use the service

- Consult, involve and work in partnership with children, young people and their families and networks to ensure that the service meets their needs.

- Design, implement and evaluate information about the service which is timely and accessible to the different needs of the community.

- Ensure that all referral procedures are followed, and that accurate assessments and signposting are performed in accordance with relevant legislation, policy and practice guidance.

- Undertake regular audits and surveys of service users'/carers' experiences, and design and evaluate activities to improve the quality of the service in response to quality issues.

- Ensure that procedures are in place for users to access and share records about their circumstances where appropriate and that all records are kept accurately and up to date in line with data protection and other relevant procedures.

- Ensure that individuals' dignity and rights are respected, through the representations and complaints procedure.

- Investigate and respond to any complaints that may be received.

- Collect, evaluate and act on information in relation to equality and diversity for children and their families and devise initiatives that promotes equality in all relationships between the service and the community.

- Ensure that the relevant professionals and agencies are worked with proactively to provide more holistic and integrated services according to the organization's policy on communication and confidentiality.

Terms and conditions

- **Minimum hours:** 40 per week between 08.00 and 19.00. You will be asked to work some unsocial hours to accommodate emergencies and planned meetings such as with Members. The service operates a time off in lieu policy.

- **Annual leave:** 35 days per annum.

- **Salary:** Scale point 45–48 negotiated on appointment.

- **Training:** You are required to undertake mandatory training in relation to the needs of the service.

- This post is suitable for job share.

This job description is intended to give the post holder an appreciation of the role envisaged and the range of duties. However, it is not exhaustive, and may be reviewed as required.

I have read and understood the above job description.

Employee's signature _____ Date _____

Employer's signature _____ Date _____

Once you have clarified the job description, the person specification should give a clear profile of the skills, knowledge, experience and aptitudes which the post holder requires to undertake the duties and role, against which subsequent criteria can be developed for recruitment. For example, Naresh will need to think about the experience, skills and knowledge that the person needs to have in order to deliver the specifics of the JD in Box 4.2. Criteria can be classified as 'essential' or 'desirable', which can help to more accurately inform decisions between applicants. The application of criteria that is 'desirable' also recognizes that there may be scope for the person to develop once in the post. This is particularly important for new roles in an organization where the provision of training can equip the post holder to develop the new skills required. This approach recognizes the value of succession planning and being active in supporting staff to develop against these requirements. For example, as services evolve an experienced social worker may wish to progress to more supervisory roles. However, it is important that all requirements are objectively justified to avoid unlawful indirect discrimination. For example, an employer should not specify that a job must be done on a full-time basis without having looked at whether it might be suitable for part-time work or job sharing. The requirement to work full-time could put women at a disadvantage compared to men because more women tend to work flexibly if they have caring responsibilities. Naresh may assume it essential to have the same person in the role, but it could be argued that the nature of the job is amenable to delegating different areas of responsibility or tasks to more than one person. Some research has demonstrated that job sharing actually has a positive impact on job satisfaction and job retention as well as advantages to employers through greater productivity (Kane 1999). Unless the employer can objectively justify a requirement for a full-time person, this is likely to be indirect discrimination because of gender or 'discrimination by association' where an applicant might be a carer for a person with what is termed in the Equality Act 2010, a 'protected characteristic' such as disability or age.

Stage 3: Developing a person specification

The person specification (PS) often involves a review of the role of the person already in the post but in the above case study Naresh will have more freedom in specifying the type of knowledge, experience, skills and qualities required. To avoid subjectivity it is best to use more than one person's view when drawing up a specification. Do not include anything in your person specification that could lead to discrimination, such as requiring something that can only be demonstrated by a single group of people with certain characteristics. Examples might include asking for someone with 'youthful enthusiasm' or somebody who is 'active and energetic'. The inclusion of unnecessary or minor requirements such as these could easily lead to discrimination by deterrence. The first example would probably be direct discrimination because of age, which the employer could not show to be objectively justified. What is actually needed is enthusiasm, but this has been stereotyped. The second example may deter people with mobility impairments, particularly if a job is mostly office based. Naresh may not even be able to specify that a driving licence is required, if limited travel is involved in the role: the best applicant for the job could easily and cheaply do the travelling involved other than by driving. This may require a 'reasonable adjustment' under the Disability Discrimination Act 1995. Therefore it would probably be discriminatory to insist on this in the specification and reject applications on the basis of lacking a driving licence. A summary of the different types of discrimination introduced by the Equality Act 2010 in relation to employment is set out in Box 4.3. You should always take advice from a qualified HR professional if in any doubt.

Of course Naresh's post of consultant social worker will need to have particular skills, experience or qualifications to do the job, leading to requirements that are objectively justified These would include a social work qualification, experience in social work with children and clear evidence of 'suitability' to work with children based on guidance from the regulatory body for social work. These must be included in what you say or write about the job and the person you are looking for, even if they exclude some people such as those with a particular protected characteristic less likely to be able to meet the requirements (Box 4.3).

Box 4.3: Terminology used in the Equality Act 2010

Protected characteristics

Age: Where this is referred to, it refers to a person belonging to a particular age (e.g. 32-year-olds) or range of ages (e.g. 18–30-year-olds).

Disability: A person has a disability if s/he has a physical or mental impairment which has a substantial and long-term adverse effect on that person's ability to carry out normal day-to-day activities.

Gender reassignment: The process of transitioning from one gender to another.

Marriage and civil partnership: Marriage is defined as a 'union between a man and a woman'. Same-sex couples can have their relationships legally recognized as 'civil partnerships'. Civil partners must be treated the same as married couples on a wide range of legal matters.

Pregnancy and maternity: Pregnancy is the condition of being pregnant or expecting a baby. Maternity refers to the period after the birth, and is linked to maternity leave in the employment context. In the non-work context, protection against maternity discrimination is for 26 weeks after giving birth, and this includes treating a woman unfavourably because she is breastfeeding.

Race: Refers to the protected characteristic of race. It refers to a group of people defined by their race, colour, nationality (including citizenship) and ethnic or national origins.

Sex: A man or a woman

Sexual orientation: Whether a person's sexual attraction is towards their own sex, the opposite sex or to both sexes.

Types of discrimination

Direct discrimination: Occurs when someone is treated less favourably than another because of a protected characteristic, they have or are thought to have.

Discrimination by association: Already applied to race, religion or belief and sexual orientation. Now extended to cover age, disability, gender reassignment and sex. This is direct discrimination against someone because they are associated with another person with a protected characteristic. (This includes carers of disabled people and elderly relatives, who can claim they were treated unfairly because of duties they had to carry out at home relating to their care work. It also covers discrimination against someone because, for example, their partner is from another country.)

Perception discrimination: Already applied to age, race, religion or belief and sexual orientation. Now extended to cover disability, gender reassignment and sex. This is direct discrimination against an individual because others think they possess a particular protected characteristic. It applies even if the person does not actually possess that characteristic.

Indirect discrimination: Already applied to age, race, religion or belief, sex, sexual orientation and marriage and civil partnership. Now extended to cover disability and gender reassignment. Indirect discrimination occurs when you have a condition, rule, policy or even a practice that applies to everyone but particularly disadvantages people who share a protected characteristic. Indirect discrimination can be justified if you can show that you acted reasonably, i.e. that it is a proportionate means of achieving a legitimate aim (reducing costs is likely to be unlawful). Being proportionate really means being fair and reasonable, including showing how you have looked at less discriminatory alternatives to decisions made.

Harassment: Unwanted conduct related to a relevant protected characteristic which has the purpose or effect of violating an individual's dignity or creates an intimidating, hostile, degrading, humiliating or offensive environment for that individual. Harassment applies to all protected characteristics except pregnancy and maternity, and marriage and civil partnership. Employees will now be able to complain of behaviour that they find offensive even if this is not directed at them and the complainant need not possess the relevant characteristic themselves. Employees are also protected from harassment because of perception and association.

Third party harassment: The Equality Act makes you potentially liable for harassment of your employees by people (third parties) who are not employees of your company such as patients, service users or contractors. You will only be liable when harassment has occurred on at least two previous occasions, you are aware that it has taken place and have not taken reasonable steps to prevent it from happening again.

Victimization: Victimization occurs when an employee is treated badly because they have made or supported a complaint or raised a grievance under the Equality Act; or because they are suspected of doing so. An employee is not protected from victimization if they have maliciously made or supported an untrue complaint.

In summary, any requirements related to what the actual job involves or to the type of person required must be directly related to a justified need. Having a clear job description and person specification, written in plain accessible language, will help to focus on these and make it less likely to become distracted by irrelevant factors, such as someone's protected characteristics. You will be more likely to get the right person for the job – the person who can do it best – as well as avoiding tribunal claims. Indeed, achieving equality and diversity in the care sector depends on the ability of individuals and whole organizations to work in ways that are respectful of individuals and assist users of the services to be as independent as possible. The person specification is an essential tool to guide staff involved in selection and recruitment. It can be used to generate a checklist for which relevant evidence to look for during the selection process. An example of what might be included in a person specification for the consultant social worker is given in Table 4.1.

Stage 4: The job advert

When advertising, the following issues should be considered:

1. Is there a local employment market, with people available with the required skills or do you need to advertise more widely? If you advertise in alternative media, you are more likely to attract applicants from marginalized groups. You could also talk to relevant local organizations to identify relevant sources or national organizations that have a circulation list.

2. Whether the post is to be advertised internally or be ring-fenced before being advertised externally. There may be equality implications if there has been a restructuring where employees adversely affected by this are entitled to apply. Senior roles attracting a certain salary may need to be advertised nationally.

3. The specialist audiences you are hoping to target and an estimate of the likely return in your choice of papers or professional publications. You need to consider where suitable applicants might look or see the advert, its relative cost and likely return (Scott *et al.* 2008).

4. Make the most of symbols which demonstrate the organization's positivity towards disabled people or those from the lesbian, gay, bisexual and transgendered community (Stonewall 2010). Include standard, positive statements in all advertisements welcoming ethnic minorities and other under-represented groups. Where there are a higher number of minority communities, consider including an advert in relevant community languages.

5. For senior posts and posts which are highly specialist you may make use of external providers to assist with recruitment such as consultants, who offer a range of services – attracting candidates, managing candidate responses, screening and shortlisting, or running assessment centres on the employer's behalf.

There are a number of methods that can be used to promote and support recruitment to your service or organizations such as:

- having an employee referral scheme, open days or tours

- developing relationships with local job centres, universities, colleges and schools to attract people into a career in social work or social care

- training staff and service users as Care Ambassadors to give presentations about work in social care

- producing a DVD or digital story to give a taster or a fuller picture of the reality of social care work

Table 4.1: Example person specification – Consultant Social Worker

	Prepared by: Naresh Bhatt Date: 16 February 2012	Job title: Consultant Social Worker Reports to: Children's Service Manager	
Specification headings	Essential	How assessed	Desirable
Experience (duration, type and level of experience necessary)	5 years post qualifying experience, 3 of which must involve statutory work with children and families setting	A	1 year or more experience of teaching, training or facilitating learning
	Evidence of formulating and implementing effective social work interventions with children, young people and their families and carers	A/T	
	Evidence of complex social work with children, young peple and their families and carers	A/I	
Qualifications (number, type and level of qualifications, or equivalent experience, if appropriate)	General Social Care Council (GSCC) recognized social work qualification	A	Teaching or training qualification (Practice Teaching, CLTHE, CIPD or equivalent)
	Registered with the General Social Care Council	A	Qualification in management or supervision (i.e. Practice Education, PG Cert Leadership and Management, NVQ or equivalent)
	Post Qualifying Award in Social Work – Children and Families	A	
	Achieved or demonstrate a willingness to work towards an approved management qualification	A/I	

Skills, knowledge and attitudes	Knowledge and understanding of child development, parenting capacity, environmental factors and risk and protective factors	A/T/I	Understanding of a range of systemic interventions and methodologies, and commitment to use of systemic approaches and social learning theory interventions.
	Knowledge of childcare legislation, statutory guidance and local child protection procedures	A/I	Knowledge of user involvement strategies in relation to children, young people and their families/carers
	Knowledge and understanding of statutory frameworks and guidance for children's social work	A/I	
	Knowledge of the roles and responsibilities of key children's agencies	A/I	
	Knowledge and awareness of issues relating to communities from different racial and cultural backgrounds and of the requirements of the Equality Act 2010	A/I	
	Knowledge of training and learning needs and ability to develop training plans and programmes of staff development	A/I	
Personal qualities and behaviours	Ability to summarize, analyse and evaluate complex information	T	
	Ability to write concise reports and have excellent written and verbal communication skills	T/I	
	Computer literacy and the skills necessary to work with information management systems and produce good quality data in a variety of formats and the ability to work with word processing packages at a speed commensurate with the responsibilities of the role	A/T	
	Ability to prioritize, monitor and be accountable for children's social work through supervision of staff	T/I	

Specification headings	Essential	How assessed	Desirable
Personal qualities and behaviours *cont.*	Ability to show leadership and understanding of the relationship approach to managing staff	A/I	
	Ability to train, support and develop staff through supervision, appraisal, coaching and mentoring	A/I	
	Proven ability to meet deadlines, manage performance and develop quality services	A/I	
	Ability to develop effective interagency working processes and networks	A/I	
	Willingness to work towards a management qualification	A/I	
Constraints	Willingness and ability to work some unsocial hours when handing over emergencies to the out of hours team (7–8pm) and to attend some planned late evening weekday meetings with Members of the Council, approximately two times per year	A/I	
Other factors (if any)	None		

A = Application form

T = Written/practical test

I = Interview

- introducing bank positions, flexible working and 'taster shifts', where appropriate, which offer opportunities for potential applicants to experience care settings before applying for jobs

- inviting potential job applicants to visit a care site for an informal chat before applying for a job – this discourages applications from non-genuine applicants.

Advertisements, whether online or on paper, should be clear and indicate the:

- requirements of the job (the specifics)

- essential and desirable criteria for job applicants in order to limit the number of inappropriate applications received (the specifics)

- nature of the organization's activities (the selling features)

- job location (the selling features)

- reward package (the selling features)

- job tenure (e.g. contract length)

- details of how to apply.

Organizations are making increased use of e-recruitment techniques by dealing with applications online, using the internet and intranet. Technology can also be used to manage the application process, storing candidate details and generating responses to applications. However, remember that you must make reasonable adjustments during the recruitment process and provide and accept information in alternative formats. For instance, if all applications have to be completed online, this will exclude those without access to a computer and broadband or those who for reason of disability are not able to use online tools.

Once the advert has been placed there must be a reliable system to deal with prospective applicants and to respond to any enquiries, for example, if you have invited informal contact, do not do this before going on leave so that equity is ensured. For many applicants this might be their first contact with your organization and you want to give a good impression and stimulate their interest (Scott *et al.* 2008, p.113). Unfair and unequal treatment of applications can occur inadvertently at this stage. The type of advert that Naresh might design based on the above guidance is illustrated in Figure 4.2.

Stage 5: Dealing with applicants

Application forms allow for information to be presented in a consistent format, and therefore make it easier to collect information from job applicants in a systematic way and objectively assess the applicants' suitability for the job. Application forms should be appropriate to the level of the job. Even if these are standard for your organization, it is worth reviewing them, as a poorly designed application form can mean applications from good candidates are overlooked, or that candidates are put off applying. For example, devoting lots of space to 'present employment' may disadvantage a candidate who is not currently working. Under the Disability Discrimination Act 1995 you must offer application forms in different formats. The recruitment process is not just about employers identifying suitable employees. It also allows applicants to find out more about your organization and whether it is one where they would like to work. Their experiences (both positive and negative) at each stage will impact on their view of the organization.

Sunshine Children and Young People's service – Consultant Social Worker
£36 – 40k, Permanent.
(Applications close 28 May 2012)

Based in an inner London, Sunshine has restructured its services in response to what children, young people and their families have told us what they really need. Building on our systems model, you will show leadership and manage the Initial Response Team's activity, provide professional consultation and training to a range of professionals and partner agencies on safeguarding issues. A registered social worker with at least 5 years experience including 3 years in children's services and a PQ in Children's Specialist Social Work, you will help develop and implement our safeguarding policies and procedures, and develop other professionals and ensure that initial assessments and pathways of families using the initial response service perform to a high standards. As the post involves training and education, a qualification or relevant experience in this area is desirable. You will need to have a sound knowledge of child development, preferably using systemic methodologies, and current issues in this area. We will offer you good supervision, support and a stake in developing our service. Our communities are diverse and therefore we welcome applicants from a range of ethnic, religious, racial and cultural backgrounds. ★Stonewall DIVERSITY CHAMPION
For informal information contact Ted Letchfield on 111 321
who will also advise on how to apply. See website www.sunshine/consultant

---

Figure 4.2: Example advert – Consultant Social Worker

Stage 6: Shortlisting

In Box 4.4 the last column identifies clearly to the applicant and the assessor of their application which criteria will be used for shortlisting and is a guide to applicants as to the evidence they need to provide against each essential criteria. Time should be taken to create a shortlist of applicants that is as objective as possible and involves all of those involved in the decision making. Given that Naresh has the appropriate background 'expert' knowledge of social work with children and families, he is possibly the best person for leading the recruitment process. Any gaps in the applicants' information should be noted so that accurate feedback can be given to those who were unsuccessful. There should be a realistic timescale between shortlisting and interviewing so that sufficient notice is given to those who need to prepare for the selection process.

Stage 7: Interviewing and assessment

Most care organizations use tests in recruitment. It is becoming more common to undertake some form of psychometric assessment for senior management posts, where making the wrong selection decision can have especially significant consequences. Tests should be used to highlight applicants' strengths and potential as well as their performance in relation to the specific requirements of the role. For example, it would be appropriate for Naresh's selection panel to test the applicants' decision-making skills under pressure by designing an 'in-tray test', and their knowledge of legislation and policy in relation to safeguarding children through a case study. The panel may ask the applicant to prepare a presentation on how they might develop the service in its first year, during which they can demonstrate knowledge about the policy context and their own ability and potential. If the applicant is asked to complete a test or a pre-interview questionnaire, they should receive a clear explanation of what is involved, why it is being used and what will happen with the results. Someone on the British Psychological Society's Register of Occupational Testers or a chartered psychologist can provide advice on whether the particular tests and the way they are being used are appropriate. It is always good practice in any testing procedure to provide participants with feedback on their results. Where these are held on file, the applicant can make a request under the Data Protection Act to see the results if they are not given feedback on request. Given that some 16 per cent of the working age population in the UK have a disability, assessing people for employment using psychometric and other tests makes it imperative that selection procedures using tests are balanced with the need for effective assessment of someone with a disability and the requirements of the Disability Discrimination Act (1995). This requires knowledge of relevant disability issues, knowledge of testing, appropriate testing policy, procedures and processes and a flexible approach. Again, it is essential to access expertise and to ensure the following areas are covered:

- Reasonable adjustment is made to the test process for disabled applicants and they know who to contact regarding requests for these.

- The selection panel is trained to interpret the results against the criteria being measured.

- The test is necessary to assess the criterion that needs to be met.

- Appropriate training is provided for all test users and other recruiters.

- There are sufficient resources to support tests through use of experts, advisors and special equipment.

Stage 8: Interviewing

Where reasonable to do so, you should try to be flexible with interview times and days, avoiding significant religious times (e.g. Friday after sunset – which may be unsuitable for an observant Jewish candidate). The person specification in Table 4.1 identified in its last column exactly which evidence against each criterion will be assessed at the planned interview. Asking for evidence in the application form or in an interview, and testing these by other means enable the panel to 'triangulate' evidence, thus increasing its reliability. Time and effort should be put into designing appropriate interview questions that enable the applicant to give information against specific criteria. For example, it may not be necessary to hear about the applicants' qualifications and experience having seen their application form but this is often a good warm up question to allow the applicant to provide more relevant or diverse information and to build rapport. Open and specific questioning should be used to get the best out of the applicant by giving them the opportunity to demonstrate what they have to offer, particularly in the areas of skills, knowledge and attitudes and allows you to get a sense of their personal qualities and behaviours, which are more difficult to assess. It is also an opportunity to check consistency of the written and oral information provided by probing and asking the 'what', 'why', 'when', 'who' and 'how' questions. For example, Naresh's panel might ask 'Tell us what you consider to be important in leading a new team and what measures would you put in place to ensure that the team worked well together in the first month of the post?' This could generate a range of evidence against different criteria on the person specification. Interviews should also be a two-way process, so giving the interviewee ample opportunity to expand or ask their own questions should be part of the process. Most organizations use a set interview format and require all panel members to be competent by completing a recruitment and selection training programme based on the organization's own standards. As chair of the panel Naresh will need to ensure equal participation of panel members throughout the process. Key issues for any interview should include:

- Ensuring that the selection panel is representative and without bias and, where this is not feasible, to ensure that the process is observed and documented by a HR professional.

- Planning, pacing and timing of interviews. The panel will not be able to be fair to applicants if interviewing more than 4–6 applicants per session.

- Thoughtful location and seating arrangements during the interview.

- Arrangements for keeping a record of the interview and recording verbal feedback from interviewers, including an agreed method used for 'ranking' applicants' responses. Interview notes must be kept for 12 months should someone wish to make a complaint and ask to see these.

- Ensuring that questions are asked consistently, accurately and get the best out of the candidate.

- Answering candidates' own questions and providing information about the post and organization as requested.

- Coordinating the decision-making process and providing information that can be appropriately used to give candidates feedback.

The selection process involves those on the selection panel exercising judgements; however, these judgements must be based on objective evidence and standardized criteria. The selection process must be developed using standardized, benchmarked and quantifiable selection tools against which to score applicants at each stage of the selection process in an equal manner. Candidates who consider that they have been discriminated against in recruitment and selection on the grounds of their race, sex, disability, sexual orientation or religion or belief, or refused employment on the grounds of membership or non-membership of a trade union, may make a claim to an employment tribunal. If the tribunal finds in the applicant's favour it may award compensation or recommend some other course of action to reduce or stop the effect of any discrimination.

Stage 9: Making decisions

Throughout the process you should keep detailed records that illustrate how decisions were made at each stage according to procedure and against criteria. Your interview records will demonstrate the quality of evidence demonstrated against each method used. This could be from the application form, the test and the interview process. It is standard to use a numeric based score such as: 1 = does not meet the criteria, 2 = partially meets criteria, and so on. Decisions should involve all members of the panel and be made as objectively as possible. Selection decisions should not be made until all the scheduled interviews have taken place. If interview panel members are not able to make detailed notes during the interview, they should independently score their responses on a standard form before comparing these with other panel members' responses. Making a selection decision must take into consideration all the assessments completed, for example any tests or presentations, and the candidates's suitability for appointment must be assessed by looking at how they have met the overall criteria. Sometimes there will need to be a ranking process and as Chair, Naresh will need to record a detailed summary of the selection panel's decision.

Collaboration in recruitment and selection starts right at the beginning with Stage 1 above, even if these tasks are delegated to Naresh and others. Collaborative planning and involvement of panel members throughout the process will reduce the potential for conflict or disagreement about selection. Seeking feedback from panel members will also facilitate continuous improvement. Skills in negotiation and managing conflict are discussed in Chapter 7.

Stage 10: Assessing suitability

'Suitability' for a post in social work and social care is a multi-faceted concept and is regulated and guided by the bodies such as the Independent Safeguarding Authority in England and the registration body. There are three key areas that underpin safe recruitment practice: criminal records and barring process, health and medical checks, and character references. Under the Care Standards Act 2000 the registration and regulatory body is required to be satisfied of an applicant's good character and conduct and considers any history of criminal matters and disciplinary records in relation to the protection of children and people who use social care services. The research around these issues has found that variation in decision making still exists. This relates to managers' lack of robust knowledge of the legislation, guidance and training, and ambiguity in the guidance itself as well as lack of consensus on what constitutes problematic offending or heavy reliance on personal opinions (Fletcher 2003; Smith 1999). Further, factors such as agency values or beliefs or the ways that agencies will be perceived by the general public and the potential response from governing bodies have been identified as being responsible for variable decision making (Perry 2004), with powerful and complex relationships between decision making and the outcomes of decisions made (Mustafa 2008). This points to the need for very structured recruitment procedures, particularly around decision making, the importance of accurate information and access to expert and legal advice, to avoid the potentially devastating consequences such decisions can have on the lives of vulnerable people.

In relation to health and medical checks, most employers issue a health questionnaire to all successful job applicants, but applicants are not required to undergo a medical examination unless they have a condition which may be relevant to the job or to the working environment. For example, if the person who is being considered for the consultant social worker post had a history of mental illness Naresh would be justified in asking the person to have a medical examination, provided it is restricted to assessing the implications for how it might impact on his ability to manage the team, particularly during crisis and in coping with stress. Naresh may be required to consider whether any reasonable adjustments could be made to reduce stress caused by the working environment, for example by offering the applicant more regular supervision or mentoring and ensuring that work patterns provide opportunities for rest and relaxation. Likewise, references should not be made part of the selection process to ensure that decisions are based on the JD, PS and the evidence provided. Selection panels should not be influenced by other factors such as potentially subjective judgements from referees. It is recommended that references should only be obtained, and circulated to members of the selection panel, after a selection decision has been reached. Having an accurate JD and PS makes it more likely that the referee focuses on the information they have about the applicant that is relevant to the job.

Stage 11: Giving candidates feedback

Feedback is an essential but often neglected part of the recruitment and selection process. The giving and receiving of critical constructive feedback has an important place in promoting self-esteem and self-improvement where candidates need to leave with a strong sense of satisfaction and security about the way their experience has been handled by your organization. Becoming aware of your own style of giving feedback is an art and needs to be practised regularly and based on clear rules. Informing candidates of how and when you will provide feedback highlights the importance of preparation and the opportunity to acknowledge or consider the power issues involved, particularly where they have been unsuccessful. You should also be prepared to receive as well as give feedback so that the organization can learn more about its reputation and standing in the community.

There may be other motives for asking for feedback than to encourage improvement, and you should be aware of this. The following format can be useful:

- Give feedback as soon as possible after the event and create the right environment for active listening.

- Thank the candidate for applying and acknowledge the time and effort made.

- Give the candidate an opportunity to say how they thought it went and what they did well or not so well as this is a more empowering approach.

- Make your feedback as objective and concrete as possible and base it on how well the candidate met or did not meet the criteria. For example, do not start to comment on their attitude but remain focused on the evidence provided and its source.

- Use specific statements such as, 'It was good when you... because...' or, 'You did not provide sufficient evidence... because..." (Kadushin and Harkness 2002, pp.160–1). This 'keep/change' rule by being more specific and letting the person know what they are already doing well and what they could change enables the candidate to receive affirming statements about themselves as well as keeping the discussion open.

- Doel, Shardlow and Sawden (1996) remind us that we should invite candidates to give us some feedback on their experiences of the recruitment process and to acknowledge this in terms of making improvements in future recruitment activities.

Monitoring equality in selection and recruitment

Finally, organizations in social work and social care are involved in monitoring the diversity of their job applicants. This may include aspects of the various protected characteristics – someone's age, disability, race, sex, pregnancy or maternity status, gender reassignment, marriage or civil partnership status, religion or belief, and sexual orientation. This information should not be seen by those responsible for making decisions about whom to shortlist or select. An exception to this is the requirement to ensure that disabled applicants who meet the minimum requirements for the post are shortlisted, or where positive action measures are being used in recruitment for a particular job. The application form should make this clear and ask for the relevant information. Monitoring can be used by an employer to see who has applied for the job and who has been selected. This information can be used to highlight any groups which are not coming forward to work for the organization or that are not being shortlisted. Information can be compared against a profile of the local or national population and show the employer where their practices may need to be improved. Some of the skills that Naresh will need to draw on to complete the recruitment and selection process, such as chairing the interview panel meeting (see Chapter 5) and involving service users (see Chapter 6) are considered in other chapters of this book.

Chapter summary

The quality of any service delivered by a social care organization is directly linked to the skills, knowledge, expertise, values and attitudes of the people who make up the workforce. Effective selection and recruitment practice is a key part of workforce development alongside systems thinking, which enables you to see the bigger picture about the type of people, skills and knowledge needed to develop the organization's vision and strategy. Engaging relevant people in the process, such as service users, makes the most of their expertise and helps to understand what works best for them through their input to both organizational and workforce development. Organizations need to increase capacity in their recruitment and retention strategies by providing flexible work opportunities that encourage non-traditional social care employees into the workforce and develop a different range of skills for the workforce to enable them to meet changing requirements. By understanding the shape and structure of the local community you are more likely to find the right people to work with you. It does not stop there, as we will see in later chapters, as reinforcement of learning and the opportunities to practise skills and knowledge for which a person may have been recruited is as important as getting the right person in the first place.

Action checklist

1. Keep up to date with issues relating to workforce development, and the external and internal forces impacting on your service that require attention to workforce needs.

2. Ensure your recruitment and selection processes actively promote equality and diversity as well as keeping within legislative requirements.

3. Design strategies for your services that promote retention.

4. Involve the community and service users in getting the right staff for your service.

Chapter 5

Managing Meetings

Being a Smooth Operator

You go to the meetings and you don't get anything done.
Service user (quoted in Beresford *et al.* 2011, p.329)

Introduction

Meetings are expensive events. They present us with a standard means of sharing information, making decisions and getting things done at both a strategic and operational level. Managing and attending meetings potentially involves substantial commitment of one's resources and time. It is therefore well worth giving attention to how effectively you manage or participate in them. Meetings can also be fun and important venues for networking, building alliances and a means of reaping the rewards of effective communication. Surprisingly, however, we do not always give enough attention to thinking about and reflecting critically upon how we attend or run meetings within our day-to-day routine.

We suggest that there can be few meetings, if any, to which people do not need to give some prior thought and planning. This chapter aims to do just that by encouraging you to examine and reflect on the range of meetings you attend and the vital importance of setting personal, service or organizational objectives for each meeting and forum you attend. Of course, any meeting involves teamwork and so the principles of good teamwork have to be embedded within any analysis and plans to maximize the effectiveness of your meetings. We have identified a number of skills associated with managing meetings more effectively and making the most of opportunities for delegation and decision making. These include thinking about the physical environment and planning skills; skills in encouraging participation and involvement, for example the promotion of active listening; conflict resolution skills and skills in exercising power and influence during the process. As we move towards more integrated and collaborative working in social work and social care, the engagement of different stakeholders, such as service users, is vital and can be achieved through the use of different styles of meetings. Some of these latter issues will be expanded in the following chapter on user participation and involvement. We will also be focusing on managing the outcomes of meetings in relation to decision making, recording, action planning and the skills required in relation to keeping control and accountability. Finally, by drawing on a wide range of examples of meetings that occur in social work and social care, we will explore some more innovative ways of running meetings which utilize creative and arts based approaches.

> Tatyana was an organizational development manager for Sylvia Rose, a social housing trust which provided extra care facilities to Jewish older people. She was called upon to help the Senior Management Team improve their monthly meetings. Over the last year, the agenda had become ridiculously long and far too operational in nature and Margaret, the Chair of Sylvia Rose, was frustrated that there was never any time available for reflection or feedback on the overall progress and development of the organization. Margaret approached Tatyana to help them incorporate some aspects of team development into their meetings so that they could move more toward being a 'learning organization'. The lack of productivity in their meetings was also something that had been picked up in recent exit interviews of staff from Sylvia Rose.

Planning meetings and the practical issues

Meetings, whether formal or informal, are an integral part of the organization's structure and activity. It may be that in your management role you are involved in both chairing and attending meetings, both of which require common yet distinct skills. The growing complexity of decision making and allocating resources within social work and social care, which often involves engaging with partners in multiple layers and guises, relies on meetings and forums being conducted efficiently and effectively. The promotion of partnership working and interprofessional cooperation in social care through the coming together of its key players has the added benefit of potential for sharing knowledge and pooling expertise. Some of these outcomes can contribute to what Margaret referred to above as the 'learning organization'. How this potential is recognized and facilitated correlates with the skill with which any meeting is conducted. Even small improvements to the effectiveness of your meetings can lead to considerable savings in time and other resources. The quality of decision making and the efficiency with which your core business is conducted can also affect working relationships outside the meeting and the credibility or reputation of the organization and the way it operates in the future. Finally, if you are involved in chairing or managing meetings, then observing the effectiveness of your performance or exercising the opportunity to observe others in meetings are all valuable learning experiences. The first thing that Tatyana suggested to Margaret, for example, was that she should come along to the next meeting and observe what was happening or not happening there. This enabled her to give some feedback and set some objectives in improving the quality of the meeting structure at Sylvia Rose.

Thompson (2006, p.83) highlights several areas in which poorly managed meetings may be wasteful, citing the multiplication of time costs. For example, in the above scenario, ten managers attend a regular monthly three-hour meeting. If this is felt to produce no benefits, there is considerable cost in terms of salaries alone. There are also a number of other costs such as preparation time, travel costs, venue hire or refreshment costs, not to mention the opportunity costs if no progress is made. These multiple costs do not include the additional but invisible costs of bad feelings and demotivation that may emerge later and get in the way of making progress with the issues confronting the Sylvia Rose Trust. The most significant costs of poorly managed meetings, however, will be seen in the effects on the experiences of service users and their networks, particularly as meetings provide a vehicle on which service users and carers depend.

Preparing for and arranging meetings
Obtain practice evidence from observation
The first step you can adopt towards reflecting on how you might improve your meetings is to make some observations during and after the next meeting you attend. As Tatyana suggested in the scenario above, you could also ask someone you trust or a coach or mentor to observe the way in which you conduct your own meetings and to provide some constructive feedback. The template in Table 5.1 offers a basic tool

which could be used for recording outcomes from this exercise. You may also wish to develop your own tool in relation to the specific skills identified for attention.

Table 5.1: 'On the Spot' – Recording your observation of a meeting

	Yes	No	Comments	Suggestions for improvement
Was the meeting effective?				
Were the intended objectives clear?				
Were the outcomes clarified or measurable?				
Was I (or somebody else) effective in the meeting and did I (or they) make a worthwhile contribution?				
Did my presence at the meeting make a difference?				
Did I (or x, y) do anything particularly well or demonstrate good practice?				
Were there any sticking points where I (or x, y) could have done things differently?				

Choosing a venue and venue layout

One of the things that struck Tatyana following her first observation was that meetings were always held at the headquarters of Sylvia Rose. Given that the ten supported housing schemes were all scattered within a 200-mile radius, this meant that some scheme managers had to travel much further than others, which became a disincentive if competing amongst other pressing demands on their time. Tatyana noted that whilst Margaret was familiar with the individual schemes where she conducted management supervision, there were few opportunities for those others she managed to 'get a feel' for the organization as a whole by visiting its different locations. In an age of austerity and increasing technology where teleworking and hot-desking are common, providing appropriate locations for meetings has become more of a challenge in social work and social care where meeting space is at a premium. One of the recommendations cited in the service user literature on how to promote equality and engage users in larger meetings is that these should be held in different venues on a rotating basis. They should include neutral ground or places that are familiar to local people and avoid seating arrangements that reflect a boardroom image. For example, public meetings and consultations may be held in venues where seats are arranged in a row facing a front table. The type of room or layout, seating arrangements and whether you need to control where people seat or allow choice should be considered in advance. This could include a more informal style by using the world cafe or round table method, grouping tables together in different areas of the room, which facilitates small group work. We will be introducing you to some different options for such meetings in the latter half of this chapter which might support more informal and creative ways of working. For formal meetings you may also give consideration as to whether a pre-meeting is needed, perhaps to form a caucus or gain commitment and momentum. This is common practice with preparing service users and carers for participating in formal or challenging forums to ensure more equal distribution of power and to increase involvement.

The level of formality

Meetings can vary in their proceedings, such as a very formal meeting with locally elected councillors for example, or where there are legal issues to attend to such as in a case conference. Less formal meetings may occur in the course of project work, or in the style of impromptu supervision or consultation with staff. Whatever the type of meeting, Rees and Porter (1996, pp.370–1) suggest that participants are aware of the business being conducted and we have elaborated on some of their headlines below.

Thinking through procedural arrangements

Procedures may be formally embedded in the constitution of the meeting or its terms of reference, for example in relation to panels constituted to agree resources after a professional case presentation which culminates in decision making. In some cases decisions may be imposed by one party, as in meetings concerning safeguarding vulnerable people where a crime has been committed. Lack of clarity about authority and in which circumstances decisions can be made collaboratively or autonomously has been raised by public enquiries into safeguarding issues (Stanley and Manthorpe 2004). The procedural arrangements may equally be agreed by those present and participating. Making sure that the right people are present at meetings cannot be overemphasized as it may be that people attend a meeting merely out of habit or a misplaced sense of duty even where they have little to contribute or gain. Likewise, if the right people are absent the outcomes or objectives may end up being unachievable (Thompson 2006) and even result in dangerous practice or prolonged delay of support to vulnerable people.

Controlling the process during meetings

Here we refer to the interpersonal skills required to manage interaction between those present at the meeting. For meetings to be effectively handled there needs to be constructive management of these interactions, for example the engagement of users/carers and staff in meetings in relation to decision making about meetings or reviewing users' support needs. Whilst the person chairing the meeting should be in control of the process, they also need to be actively constructive in managing the interaction between those present. Tatyana, for example, observed that Margaret tended not to allow any silences as she was so focused in getting through a demanding business agenda in the time available. The potential for substantial power dynamics has been well documented (Cook 2010), which means giving attention to communication skills such as empathy, authenticity and respect, as well as being able to summarize, reflect throughout the process and communicate any decisions made within the time available. Even in more informal situations, such as an impromptu consultation with staff over the photocopier, there should always be a process aspect to the discussions. The skill with which these aspects are handled can affect the quality and acceptability of any outcome.

One of the exercises that Tatyana asked Margaret to do was to make a plot of the interactions in her meeting using what we know about genograms in social work and social care. A genogram is a pictorial display of a person's or group of people's relationships and allows the creator to identify patterns, particularly repetitive patterns, or to explore power dynamics. Adapting method associated with genograms makes it possible through observation or reflection to plot the interactions and dynamics that happen in meetings. Figure 5.1 shows a simple version of Margaret's post-meeting 'plot', in other words, what she recollected from the first 15 minutes of her last group meeting. Margaret was chairing the meeting and is represented in Figure 5.1 by the 'smiley' face. What Margaret quickly realized was that the manager sitting opposite her tended to be very challenging and spoke only to her directly, which she then tried to ignore by minimizing her responses but with little success. More surprisingly, Margaret realized that some people in her meeting were regularly not contributing and were similarly marginalized by others. Margaret was then able to adapt her analysis further by using some of the colour-coded lines and symbols commonly used in genograms to represent the different emotions or behaviours being observed and experienced in her meetings (see Figure 5.2 for a range of these) to achieve a more in-depth analysis of how the participants might be relating to one another. Reflecting on these together with Tatyana helped Margaret to focus on her own interpersonal skills and strategies for guiding and managing interactions more effectively in her meetings.

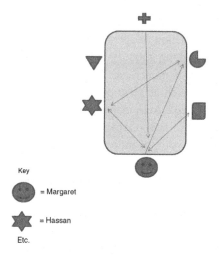

Key

● = Margaret

✡ = Hassan

Etc.

Figure 5.1: Plotting and analyzing meetings

Z_____X	Active	Z.................X	Indifference or apathy
Z>>>>>>>>X	Engaged/ participative	Z========X	Discord or conflict
Z************X	Enthusiastic	Z ~~~~~~~~X	Distrust/suspicious
Z++++++++X	Supportive	Z_____II_____X	Angry or hostile
Z - - - - - - - -X	Neutral	ZmmmmmmmX	Manipulative or controlling

NB: Use different colours to depict different types of emotions and develop your own symbols to make them more familiar and easy to use.

Figure 5.2: Suggested symbols to use in genograms to depict interactions in meetings

Staying with the substantive content or task

Rees and Porter (1996) refer to this as the 'main business of the meeting' (p.370), bringing together the above procedural and process arrangements. For example, you may sometimes have to identify those issues that arise which may not be substantive to the business of the meeting, if those present are not able to make decisions or act upon them. These should be followed up outside the meeting. Preparing and stating the structure for the meeting should indicate the time allocated and required in order to address its substantive issues or tasks and this is normally the main function of agenda setting. However, one should try to be proactive in thinking about how these are ordered and the degree of freedom afforded, if immediate decisions need to be taken. Often in regular meetings, such as team or management meetings, there is a volume of work that needs to be managed. Consideration should be given to combining items and to the logic of sequencing, as well as allowing enough time for discussion of individual items on the agenda. It is too easy to spend an inordinate amount of time on easy and relatively minor items with key issues being left to the end when participants are tired or have to leave early. Some consideration therefore should be given to varying the order of the agenda if necessary. When chairing a meeting you should be aware of participants raising items on the back of others instead of tabling them beforehand or using the meeting as a dumping ground for issues where responsibilities lie elsewhere or for problems that the meeting cannot resolve. This calls for skills in reflection in action (Schön 1987). One of the issues Margaret had with the meetings of Sylvia Rose was in making space for the bigger developmental tasks facing the organization. One of the suggestions that Tatyana could make to Margaret is to identify a single topic which needs a more in-depth or developmental approach. For example, thinking about what it means for Sylvia Rose to be a 'learning organization', lends itself to facilitating a more creative type of meeting, using some of the alternative methods outlined towards the end of this chapter.

Purposes of meetings

We have already distinguished between formal and informal meetings. We encouraged you to reflect upon the different types of meetings you attend either regularly or less frequently. You may wish to go back to the reflective exercise in Table 2.1 (Chapter 2) where you identified how you spend your time. This may remind you of how much time you actually spend in meetings and the follow-up work required. Rees and Porter (1996) identify some examples of types of meetings which we have elaborated upon in relation to those common to social care:

- fact finding (case conferences/inspection and audit/evaluation)
- exchange of views (team development/learning events/appraisal)
- negotiating (meetings with commissioners and providers/trade unions or HR)
- consultation (meetings with service user forums/supervision/ strategy meetings)
- briefings (team meetings/management meetings/formal presenta- tions)
- problem-solving (supervision/case conferences/strategy meetings)
- 'bonding' or networking (peer group meetings/social events/ working lunches).

However, we have found that the more you try to classify meetings, the more broad or specialized they become. For example, there is a lot of potential cross-over in the above categories. For the purposes of this chapter, however, we have focused on three types of meeting in order to highlight some of the different knowledge and skills required, for example business or organization orientated, team or staff development orientated and service user orientated. Some of the issues discussed will be common to all three.

Business/organization orientated
ROLE OF THE CHAIR

Chairing meetings can be a daunting task; undertaking preparatory work, for example preparation of the agenda and distribution of the relevant papers or documentation is vital. Meeting in advance with the person administering can facilitate the smooth running of the meeting. You should spend some time thinking about the objectives of your meeting and clarifying these will help you prepare. It is also worthwhile thinking about what will be expected of you during the meeting and again this indicates the preparation you need to make so that other people's needs can be satisfied. You will, for example, need to be familiar with and able to explain any procedural rules likely to arise so these can be reassuringly dealt with. The chair will need to understand the substantive issues and their history sufficiently to guide the subsequent discussion.

In Chapter 2 we referred to the use of technology in enhancing communication. Technology can also be useful to overcome some of the time constraints we face in meeting time. For example, over the few weeks that Tatyana and Margaret worked together, they spoke via Skype, which saved on travelling time. Margaret explored the options of video conferencing to reduce meeting time allocated to the core business of the organization and she also had a training event for her team and herself in how to set up and manage a wiki as a means of keeping debates alive on the key issues in the organization in between meetings. A wiki is a website in which you can give invited members and those authorized with editing rights to add or change material on the site. Margaret found this particularly useful when discussing issues around equality and diversity in Sylvia Rose. She found that her staff team was more likely to contribute spontaneously as issues arose and share examples of good practice and challenges. She was also able to disseminate research evidence and share policy documents in progress via the wiki. Previous to this she had always experienced a silence when the agenda item 'equal opportunities' was routinely placed at the end of the meeting agenda and this had felt very tokenistic. By using a wiki Margaret was able to engage her staff in more of an active discourse on what 'equal opportunities' really meant to Sylvia Rose.

NOTES OR MINUTE-TAKING

Notes or minutes can be very influential later on. This may be a legal or formal requirement and having someone take the minutes independently may be of great value to the person chairing so that they are free to concentrate on important issues that need attention. Meeting minutes have no value if they are not accurate. Names and terms, especially the organization's own jargon, must be used carefully, particularly if you are involving service users. A good minute-taker will prepare ahead of the meeting and if you are chairing the meeting it is worth spending time to ensure that they have the opportunity to review related documents, such as minutes from previous meetings, or any other papers related to the topic. In care settings, because of the squeeze on administrative support, it may be necessary to engage a participant in the meeting in taking minutes. This is often left to spontaneity, and can affect the quality of the minutes provided, so again it is worth agreeing some key points about what should be noted or minuted and timescales for when and how they will be distributed (preferably whilst the meeting itself is still fresh in people's minds). Sometimes it can take organizations days or even weeks to complete and circulate meeting minutes. A delay in circulating meeting minutes usually means a delay in taking action. Prompt meeting minutes are likely to be not only more accurate but more effective. A hallmark of good minutes is providing the right balance between in-depth coverage of complex topics and providing a concise summary of the key issues and decisions taken. Style should vary according to the purpose to which the minutes will be put. Depending on the purpose, the right choice for minutes can vary from a very concise summary to a word-for-word transcript of what was said and by whom. Designing a template might help, particularly if note-taking is done by a more informal arrangement. The depth of coverage should always be agreed in advance. A good meeting often brings together people who have interesting ideas and a lot to say, and sometimes this means that debates can get contentious, even heated. Neutral, objective minute or note-taking is all the more important in the face of controversy. You can always make your own aide memoire alongside formal minutes.

DELEGATION

Meetings provide an important structure and process for delegation where you may assign or be assigned responsibility for specific outcomes or tasks on behalf of an individual, usually somebody senior to you or for the team or organization. Delegation can be temporary or permanent and is more than sharing out jobs but usually involves recognizing that the person to who you are delegating has some autonomy, depending on their existing knowledge and level of skill. Delegation also provides a learning or professional development opportunity where you may give more support and be more involved in supervision. Many researchers (Harris 1998; Lawler and Bilson 2010) including the Social Work Task Force (DCSF 2009) have documented the lack of autonomy and motivation perceived by those working in social care as a result of increased managerialism and the overt wielding of power from a position of authority and defensiveness. Many motivational theories point to the importance of accountability and responsibility in determining how staff behave and respond, and delegation can be a way of enabling them to feel more involved and engaged if they feel they are being trusted with important responsibilities or activities. These are issues relevant to Chapter 4 on recruitment and selection; managers who think they are perfect or strong (Hay 2009) will be less likely to delegate. This was the case for Dominique in Chapter 2. Staff who are encouraged to think and reflect upon the tasks they are asked to do, and invited to engage in the process of considering alternatives and making choices, are much more likely to find their work more rewarding.

The allocation of tasks from meetings is not to be confused with delegation as there is a subtle and important distinction. Responsibility and accountability are important. What Margaret realized when she was encouraged to review her meetings with Tatyana, was that she thought it was easier to do most of the 'important' tasks herself in the belief that 'it is quicker'. You may find it timely to return to your time management audit (see Table 2.1) and review which work can be delegated and to whom. Can this be permanent or just temporary? As you have been reading this book you may have realized that given the range of demands on managers it is impossible to do everything, and if you are experiencing an uneven workload a review of the delegations in place is warranted. Returning to delegation during meetings, the task delegated could be related to the organizational structure, for example, in relation to Naresh's appointment of a consultant social worker in the previous chapter, he was able to delegate all the key tasks associated with this new role. Effective delegation is an important leadership skill and effective leaders use delegation to balance workloads and provide staff development opportunities. After a discussion with the person who appeared not to contribute to her staff meetings, Margaret could use delegation to encourage more active contribution and feedback that would be motivating and reinforced by constructive feedback from other members of her team.

Team or staff development orientated
CREATIVE MEETINGS FOR TEAM BUILDING AND SUPPORTING LEARNING

Effective meetings are all about teamwork, and the quality of your meetings will inevitably reflect the stage of group development. Wheelan (2010, pp.26–32) identifies the different stages of development as follows, on which we have elaborated to illustrate how people may respond in meetings:

- *Stage 1: Dependency and inclusion.* This is characterized by group members' dependency and concerns about feeling safe and included. Meetings where people are not expressing different points of view or engaging in decision making may be in this stage.

- *Stage 2: Counter dependency and fighting.* As the group becomes focused on its key task, conflict may emerge and the group can become stuck. Being active in resolving conflict (see Chapter 7) can help to unify the group's view of its purpose and procedures so that collaboration can be achieved.

- *Stage 3: Trust and structure.* If the group has achieved Stages 1 and 2, its members will begin to cooperate more and communication becomes more open. Professional territoriality decreases and group meetings may be characterized by more positive working relationships through negotiations and procedures – now is your time to delegate perhaps?

- *Stage 4: Work.* Members show energy, productivity, commitment and effectiveness, and the quality and quantity of the work increases significantly. Wheelan asserts that some people may never experience this stage in their teams, but this stage reflects what Margaret expects if her organization is to become a 'learning organization'. Teams and meetings who are at 'work' may fluctuate but generally proceed in a positive direction. Here it is important to keep your eye on changes in membership, external demands and changes in leadership as these may affect the work of the group. Regression may occur and necessitate the rebuilding of the group structure and culture.

Teams or groups do not just develop without a bit of help, encouragement and direction from you. Managers need to learn about group development and acknowledge that developing a team or group requires skill – not just your own, but capitalizing on the skills and motivations of others. In this section we offer a few suggestions for being more creative with your meetings, by taking occasional time out to pay attention to the development of the group whilst still working towards your goal or key task. These are experiential methods and are summarized in Table 5.2.

Table 5.2: Methods for more creative meetings

Method/style	Suitable for	How to prepare or run
World Café Method (see www. peopleand participation. net/display/ Methods/ World+Cafe)	For hosting a large group dialogue on a problem or issue for the service.	1. Lay out the environment cafe style, setting tables for four to six people. Leave an item on the table to get people talking together before the formal discussions. 2. Welcome and introductions, put people at ease, set the context and aims. 3. Small group rounds. Give each table a question to discuss relevant to the main topics or issues After 15–20 minutes encourage individuals to move to another table to discuss the same question with a different group. 4. Expand questions as people move around so you are building up perspectives and feeding conversations. Appoint a host for each table whose job it is to summarize the overall discussion. 5. After a number of rounds, encourage groups to share insights with the large group and capture this using flip-chart, post-it notes or notes taken by the host.

Open Space Technology (attributed to Owen 2008)	Based on systems thinking, this is suitable for encouraging participants to identify issues for which they have a real passion and which they are willing to take responsibility for. Those who join the group for discussion are the right people – they attend because they care about it. Whatever comes out is the only thing that could have done as it deals with the issue in the moment. Never think that you are in charge. Informed by distributive and participatory leadership practice.	1. Issue a broad, open invitation that articulates the purpose of the meeting. 2. Arrange participant chairs in a circle. 3. Provide a 'bulletin board' on which participants can post their issues and opportunities. 4. Create a 'marketplace' with many breakout spaces that participants move freely between, learning and contributing as they 'shop' for information and ideas on the issues they are most interested in. 5. Provide time out between small-group breakout sessions. 6. Get feedback from participants leading their 'issues' in a plenary which takes the form of suggesting solutions.

Service user orientated
SETTING STANDARDS FOR INVOLVING SERVICE USERS IN MEETINGS

We have made frequent references in this book to the role that service users play in working alongside managers and their needs to develop skills and knowledge if their roles are to be valued. This will form the basis for further discussion in Chapter 6. Developing some basic standards about what service users and staff can expect when attending a meeting might encourage and increase their participation. There should be minimal standards for their engagement in meetings about their support and care, for example; some of the relevant techniques, skills and methods for involving service users are discussed in the next chapter in more detail. The types of issues that users have raised themselves as being vital for their participation in meetings about them involve:

1. Being included in all the meeting when it is about them. Service users should not be excluded from parts of the meeting unless there is third party information to be discussed.

2. Having an opportunity to discuss and agree the choice of venue.

3. Sending out invitations to a meeting in their own name and being given some administrative assistance. This requires thinking about how to give plenty of notice to service users and actively planning reviews with them rather than for them.

4. Involving service users in any cancellations and subsequent rearranging of meetings particularly as they are the people who actually need to be there!

5. Having the opportunity to be able to talk through the plan for the meeting which might involve a social worker or care coordinator, or the person chairing the meeting or accompanying them, such as an advocate.

6. Being provided with advocacy where appropriate. This could be formal or informal advocacy.

7. Having the opportunity to chair the meeting if they wish to do so or at least meet and be introduced to everyone attending the meeting before, during or after.

8. Being consulted about how their views are going to be presented and the format for presenting information.

9. Being involved in how the meeting minutes are presented, particularly in meetings about their own care and support.

10. People presenting reports talking to service users directly and reflecting any complex issues to check that service users understand any jargon or background issues that are taken for granted by other people attending.

11. Making pens and paper available.

12. At the end of the meeting, having an agreement from all participants about the action plan and their individual goal or action point with clear timescales.

13. Being given a copy of the minutes in straightforward language with no jargon.

14. After the meeting being given copies of any reports referred to and having the opportunity to contribute views about anything they disagree with.

15. Having an opportunity to give some feedback about how the meeting went from their perspective.

Of course there will be times or situations where service users, carers or their representatives are not able to be present and this poses a challenge as to how to involve or represent them. Box 5.1 gives us some insight from a service user about her experience of different types of meetings. Being creative with meetings with service users is also valuable, particularly using arts-based methods to increase their engagement and to overcome more traditional barriers in communication. Hafford-Letchfield *et al.* (2010) and Hafford-Letchfield (in press) illustrate experiments, for example with using drama with older people in order to consult and engage their views about the relevance of service provision.

Box 5.1: Service user commentary

In my experience, when at meetings, the service user participants tend to cluster at one end of the meeting for moral support and sometimes because of lack of confidence or experience. The balance of power around the table tends to be, or is at times, centred on the chair of the meeting. I have observed that the agenda tends to be structured with the items of most concern to them first, so that the service users' items are placed towards the latter part of the proceedings.

When attending a meeting as an 'equal member of the team', for example, in my role as service user coordinator in a mental health trust, I have observed that the balance of power tends to be in favour of my management peers with little opportunity for service user managers, such as myself, to articulate what they are capable of. As a member of staff recruited for my expertise as a service user, I have found that there is a tendency to over-monitor people like myself, highlighting disadvantages or difficulties rather than ability.

My recommendation would be that roles and responsibilities should be rotated and training made available for participants with user experience who attend meetings on a regular basis. This can motivate and enhance one's self-esteem particularly for those service user participants who may be new to the experience of participating in social work and social care meetings.

Don't forget that the role of a service user attending meetings can be that of a management peer, a client representative or the actual client. As a management peer we can offer a dual perspective on proceedings as can those of us that are service users engaged in service user involvement activities. Involvement should be evident at all levels of proceedings except where confidentiality is an issue. Information should be disseminated to all those concerned and the meeting should accommodate different learning styles and abilities. A creative learning approach could benefit all participants such as those recommended towards the end of this chapter.

As someone who has had to learn how to give my best in meetings, I think that it is innovative to allow potential participants to observe meetings first. This enables one's confidence, encourages participation and works towards collaborative progression, thus making involvement meaningful. In my experience venue style, layout and location on occasion has been intimidating, due to a lack of confidence and experience. Smaller groups feeding back to the core group in a meeting enables participation from more members of any meeting and promotes the collaborative efforts of the delegates.

Christine Khisa

Chapter summary

'Meeting' is rather a dry word to summarize what we do in social work and social care and there are a lot more creative words to describe the process of interaction and collaboration to get the job done. Whatever style or methods are used these should involve an ever evolving cycle of communication that allows for innovation as well as clarity in the work being undertaken. It is vital to remember that 55 per cent of our communication is in fact non-verbal and the quality of interaction with our colleagues and stakeholders matters more than the frequency. This chapter has considered some of the skills involved in meetings in greater detail than our daily practice takes for granted and provided you with some useful tools with which to review your effectiveness at meetings, either as a participant or in running your own meetings. The degree of social interaction involved will also affect team working and knowledge transfer and these can be balanced with the creative thought and productive work that takes place away from the meeting space, which should be equally valued.

Action checklist

1. Regularly review your meetings and assess their effectiveness. This should relate to the aims and objectives, purpose and outcomes of all meetings, no matter how small.

2. Seek regular feedback from participants on their experiences of meetings you are responsible for.

3. Don't be afraid to experiment and use creative methods for developmental opportunities for the individuals participating in meetings.

4. Don't hold back, and delegate responsibly.

Chapter 6

Skills in Collaboration and Networking

Building up Successful Partnerships with Service Users

We have not provided services with people; we have provided them for people. Therefore our commitment has been to some kind of paternalistic socialism.
David Blunkett

I can choose my own respite facilities and check them out first to make sure they meet my needs as a disabled...person. I can control where I go and pay for it with the IB money.
Unnamed woman (quoted in Newbronner *et al.* 2011, p.68)

Introduction

This chapter is about people and the support services that all of us will turn to at some point in our lives. It is about the nature of the relationship between people and these services. Whilst it is the case that all of us have the potential to use services, our focus is on those people with long-term experience of them, for whom services are an integral part of life. All social work and social care managers will quickly encounter the debate about user involvement; indeed, making progress in this area might be one of the most valuable contributions that they can make in improving services. As practitioners they ought to have had experience of involving users in decisions about their individual support arrangements and might well, especially in adult services, have facilitated people to consider taking control of their own support. Now, as managers, they have an opportunity to think about broader levels of user involvement in the running, planning and evaluation of services.

Whilst we will argue that the debate about involvement is at heart a moral debate, there are strong arguments that it is also about quality. The Sainsbury Centre for Mental Health (2010, pp.10–11), for example, found a range of benefits that emerge from user involvement in the planning of services, including:

- improved morale (for both users and staff)
- better decision making
- better health outcomes
- more likelihood of change succeeding.

We will use the work of two managers to explore this area. We introduced Rupa in Chapter 1 and saw how she was progressing in Chapter 3 when discussing the management of change, where we heard about her ideas about improving residents' involvement in the running of a residential unit. We will return to this situation in this chapter. We will also consider the work of Sharon, below.

> Sharon manages a local authority service for young people leaving care. She has been in post for six months and wants to increase the involvement of young people in how the service is run. This is core to social work values, and senior managers in her department are keen to document progress in this area to ensure compliance with national standards. Whilst Sharon understands the importance to her department of meeting the performance requirements, she feels uneasy about just being able to 'tick boxes'. 'How', she wonders, 'can I make it a real part of my team's work that we join with young people in thinking about improving how we do things?'

Developing user involvement

In the UK context, service user participation and user involvement is the cornerstone of social care and social work policy and philosophy. People's expectations of social care services are now a significant driver of the way in which services are commissioned and provided. There is also a legal requirement for user involvement within adult and child care, family policy and practice, as well as in the community as a whole. This also reflects the broader agenda in public policy, where there has been an emphasis on a consumerist agenda (Hafford-Letchfield 2010). This is informed by increasing customer choice and consumer involvement in a mixed economy of care, based on a political and ideological shift towards the market and the purchase of services. More recently, it has moved towards more personalized and individualized commissioning. There is a belief that if service users' requirements are accurately identified then service providers can offer a more efficient and economic service. Political commitment to public participation has arisen via the devolution of local government, user involvement in public services, the recognition of human and civil rights of disabled people and combating social inclusion (Beresford and Croft 2001). Both Sharon and Rupa are among the many social work and social care managers who are committed to a democratic approach to service user involvement, which is primarily concerned with empowerment and the redistribution of power, and with people gaining more control over their lives (Hafford-Letchfield *et al.* 2008). Our own experience is that social work and social care organizations are at varying stages in addressing these issues, and that there are variations within organizations themselves. This sense of unevenness comes through strongly in the wide-ranging research on user involvement reported by Beresford *et al.* (2011), and earlier in Barnes' overview of developments in mental health services (Barnes 2002). Pearson *et al.* (2011) add to this picture of patchiness in their research into how public service organizations involved disabled people in the development of Disability Equality Duty policies, noting significant variations in practice and, in some areas, mere tokenism.

Box 6.1: 'On the Spot' – Where do we stand on user participation?

We have noted that organizations are at different points, and within organizations there will be variations. Think about your own organization. On a scale of 1 (little progress) to 10 (total participation), how would you evaluate the current position with participation? Now think of a user: would their assessment be similar to yours? Finally, think about someone in your organization's senior management team: would his or her assessment be the same as yours and the service user?

If you sense that there would be differences, how might you account for these?

Wherever you stand, skills in developing participation and partnerships now permeate all management and professional activity. In successful organizations service user involvement sits close to corporate decision-making bodies and is represented on those bodies which help to oversee service user involvement. However, some have argued (Beresford and Croft 2001) that user participation in social work and social care has predominantly been based on the consumerist agenda, relying more on methods that are bureaucratic and managerially and professionally driven. This development, they suggest, is not always successful in increasing personal and political power and ultimately the empowerment of service users, as in many ways control of the system still remains with the service or organization (Carr 2007). It is implied here that user participation is in danger of becoming a means to an end rather than an end in itself, an outcome which we should seek to avoid. Using participation as an essential tool to improve social care should promote a democratic approach emerging from service users' rights and requirements. Any participation strategies have to include more practical ways to base participation on the direct experiences and perspectives of service users and their representative organizations. Any review of developments in this area so far clearly demonstrates that service users themselves have always led, and will continue to lead, the way forward.

Towards co-production

Barnes, Mercer and Din (2003) show the importance of service users powerfully in reviewing the work of disabled people in setting up user-controlled services in the UK. They trace recent developments back to the 1960s and 1970s and the growing opposition to the paternalistic nature of services. This dissatisfaction was linked closely with the development of the social model of disability as distinct from an individualistic model (Oliver 1983). The first substantial legislative response, on the back of years of pressure from user movements, was the Community Care (Direct Payments) Act of 1996, followed by the Carers and Disabled Children Act of 2000.

The period since the 1960s has been one in which challenges to professional/provider power bases and assumptions has gathered momentum. In mental health the 1970s saw the growth of user movements critical of psychiatry. Wallcraft and Bryant (2003), reviewing the extent of mental health user groups in England, noted that the movement was expanding and becoming more influential, but was poorly resourced. Given the level of resourcing, Wallcraft and Bryant note tensions about the demands on the groups' time from statutory agencies for consultation.

The idea of children as people with rights dates from the early twentieth century, with an initial focus on rights to protection. Children's rights through history have been closely bound up with conceptions of childhood (children as 'little adults' or childhood as a period in its own right) and with arguments about their being the 'property' of fathers. As we have accepted that children are people, so the idea of their involvement in decision making has grown, now enshrined in Article 12 of the UN Convention on the Rights of the Child.

There are a number of striking things when we reflect on these developments:

- There are many voices, but the insistent and authentic voice has been that of the user.

- Control is central. 'The professional knows best' sits at a distance from 'nothing about us without us'.

- The balance and nature of power thus becomes a focus for exploring how social work and social care organizations and their staff relate to people who need their support.

- How people are defined is important. The words 'service user', 'consumer', 'client' and 'citizen' have distinctive connotations that influence approaches to participation.

- The questioning of the 'professional knows best' belief has created a whole new debate about the nature of knowledge and expertise, with the emergence, for example, of the concept of 'expert by experience'.

Reflecting on the user movement views, another thought emerges: they seem *ordinary*. Theirs is not a radical demand for an overthrowing of the state: it is pressure for equality and citizenship. In the words of the authors of *We Are Not Stupid*, 'We want what everyone wants' (Taylor *et al.* 2007, p.93). This amounts to involvement in planning and decision making about services that are central to their lives. As we will explore later, the debate is about citizenship. Brodie, Cowling and Nissen (2009) make it clear that the movements summarized above are far from peculiar to the UK, or to health and social care services. In their review of participation in public services generally, they note a global 'explosion' of interest, with citizenship at risk of being marginalized by governments' adoption of consumerist approaches to public services.

Rupa and Sharon have thus begun their careers in management when this debate about involvement remains real and lively. But are the words they use – 'partnership', 'consultation', 'collaboration', 'participation', for example – clear in meaning? Or will Rupa and Sharon mean something different from those whom they seek to involve?

> 'When I use a word', Humpty Dumpty said, in rather a scornful tone, 'it means just what I choose it to mean – neither more nor less.' (Lewis Carroll, *Through the Looking Glass*)

Service user 'involvement', 'participation', 'collaboration', 'partnership' do not belong in the language of small talk. Behind each word lie fundamental principles for contemporary social work and social care management and practice. We must treat them with care, because as Humpty Dumpty reminds us, words can be slippery and elusive. Cornwall (2008) writes of participation, for example, that it 'can easily be reframed to meet almost any demand made of it' (p.269). Help is available, however, in seeking greater clarity. Perhaps the classic analysis of participation comes from Arnstein (1969). Writing from a citizen perspective, she conceived participation as a ladder, and this idea has been adapted by a wide range of organizations, serving both adults and children (see Hart 1997, for example), which you may already be familiar with. Applying Arnsteins ladder of participation to the social work and social care sector may illustrate different levels for example, the act of informing and consulting service users and carers, through to engaging them in partnership and delegating full control of resources and decision making either as individuals or within community based user led organizations. Whilst these suggest a hierarchy in stages of user involvement it is important not to be prescriptive but to tailor this to the situations with which users are involved with.

Arnstein's central argument is that approaches to participation differ in relation to the balance of power between citizens and those with formal power. For Sharon, Rupa and their colleagues in social work and social care management, all levels except 1 and 2 will be legitimate at some point, so that the concern is to ensure that we are not fooling ourselves by thinking that, for example, we are working in partnership when in fact all we are doing is consulting. Research has demonstrated that user feedback is strong on wanting to know why involvement is sought (Involve 2005; Moriarty *et al.* 2007).

'Partnership', level 6 in Arnstein's ladder, is another word that can confuse. Banks observes that 'the term "partnerships" is increasingly losing credibility, as it has become a catch-all for a wide range of concepts, and a panacea for a multitude of ills' (Banks 2002, p.5). Arnstein helps to clarify meaning through the notion of shared decision making. Wildridge *et al.* (2004, p.4) provide some criteria through which we might judge partnerships. From their review of the literature, they argue that there are some common features in definitions. Although their focus is on partnerships between agencies, we think that their ideas transfer to user–agency partnerships in the features described below:

- common goals

- joint rights, resources and responsibilities

- an aim to improve services

- equality

- trust.

If we think about how we use the word 'partner' in our personal lives, these elements are probably important to us. The idea of 'common goals', for example, does not preclude different contributions: we all bring different skills, knowledge and perspectives into our relationships with partners. The analysis also points towards the importance of time: trust is not a quality that can be written into contracts or agreements, but needs to be gained through our behaviour.

We want to argue, based on the above, that clarity about how we are using key words must come before any attempts to develop participation and partnership. Rupa and Sharon need the skills to ensure that they are clear about what they mean by these key words. Alternatively they run the risk of talking at cross purposes.

Box 6.2: 'On the Spot' – Language and its use in my team

We have explored at some length the words commonly used in discussions about participation. Is language important to you? If so, what are the words commonly used in your team in conversations about participation? Is there agreement on what these words actually mean? It might be worthwhile raising the issue at a team meeting, given that there might be some unexplored confusion about it all. It might also be worth thinking about the language about participation used in your organization more generally. Some managers might be using the same word but meaning different things.

Examining the nature of the relationship we have with service users requires us to consider the different terms used to describe and articulate that relationship, for example 'service user', 'consumer', 'customer', 'client' or 'expert by experience' (Carr 2004, 2007; McLaughlin 2009; Simmons, Powell and Greener 2009) (see Box 6.2). Analysis of these different terms and the political and social circumstances behind their adoption highlight the hierarchical positions involved and may represent genuine moves towards participation or more consumerist discourses within social work and social care. 'Service users' is our widely used current preferred term when we are talking about people receiving support from social work and social care services. Although popular, it is still a problematic term. It suggests a narrow view of people, ignoring the reality of multiple identities – father, son, friend, partner, worker, neighbour and so on.

Table 6.1: Terminology and inferences

People as consumers	People as citizens
Choices	Rights
Consultation	Representation
Limited application	Broad application
Origins in the market	Origins in democracy

In recent years, the model of 'co-production' attempts to steer a middle path:

> The current state of consumerism within social care rests upon an uneasy synergy between highly influentia\l, articulate 'bottom-up' user movement and the 'top-down' ambitions of successive governments to increase the penetration of market-related mechanisms into the public sector. (Glendinning 2009, p.178)

Co-production emphasizes the role that service users play in both the consumption and production of public services by highlighting the interdependence of consumer–producer relationships (Needham and Carr 2009). Co-production moves beyond 'engagement' and 'participation' in that it can involve service users and their communities in being actively involved in shaping service planning and decision making, as in levels 6 and 7 in Arnstein's ladder. Further, service users can be involved in the shaping of the actual service outcomes and how to deliver them. Co-production aims to move beyond simply being invited by the professional and managerial staff to contribute ideas towards taking a more active lead in determining how services develop (Pemberton and Mason 2008). The model developed by In-Control, a national charity which campaigns for self-directed support, shows how this relationship is constantly defined between managers, professionals and service users. The exchange between people is reinforcing moving service users from dependency towards mutuality and reciprocity. The role for you as the manager in this model would be to facilitate, by contributing time, skills and ideas in order to design, deliver and improve services.

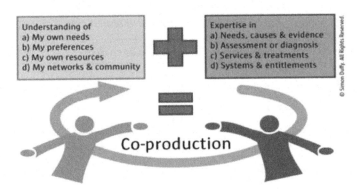

Figure 6.1: Model of co-production

Source: The Centre of Welfare (reprinted with kind permission from Reform Limited)

We hope that the exploration of these key concepts has been helpful in thinking about your current practice. A common reason for variation within and between organizations will be the tone of relationships. We turn to these now.

Relationship skills

For you, co-production is likely to take place in a more intimate setting where staff you manage are consulting with service users about their support needs and facilitating autonomy on an individual basis in partnership. The role of managers in creating forums in which common ground can be articulated and services improved emphasizes the importance of dialogue, interaction and negotiation skills with those on the ground. We want here to explore relationships in social work and social care, given that improvements in service user partnership and participation require a relationship shift. In Bell and Smerdon's literature review of relationships in public services, for example, there are powerful arguments across a range of services (Bell and Smerdon 2011). In all cases users could not judge the effectiveness of the service without reference to the quality of relationships: and collaboration was one of the identified elements of effectiveness. This is not surprising, because much of the 'business' of social work and social care is done through relationships.

The debate about labels illustrated earlier, 'glosses over some of the most fundamental issues in politics, issues with implications for the distribution of power and benefits in society and for related questions of social justice, replacing them with a simple slogan such as putting customers first' (Aberbach and Christensen 2005, p.236).

Consumers or citizens?

Let us take Sharon's commitment to involving young people leaving care in the service. She will need to be clear which 'label' she is attaching to the young people concerned. Are they consumers or citizens? Either might be appropriate, but each will lead her in its own direction. As 'consumers' of the service, they might be consulted on what the service is doing well and what it needs to improve. As 'citizens', they might be given more shared decision-making responsibilities over what the service does. There is, in real world terms, an overlap between the two, but the key distinction, in Arnstein's terms, will be in relation to who has power. Simmons (2009) questions whether users of public services want to become consumers and whether this stance is a sufficient lever for diffusing power? More significantly, although there has been a big increase in the discourse of consumerism and choice, this does not necessarily mean that users have more consumer mechanisms. Simmons argues that whilst there are now many different dimensions of choice, the most frequent use of the term relates to choice of location or type of services. She also argues that consumers have to be informed about the choices before them as well as to be willing and able to make choices. Therefore there are many potential problems with choice in the public sector and whilst Sharon is required by her organization to send signals that choice stimulates the best services and leads to progressiveness, it might also lead to increased inequality if some of the young people in her service are not able to exercise choice. In the wider field of user involvement there is no doubt about the model preferred: that of citizenship (Beresford *et al.* 2011; Moriarty *et al.* 2007). The wish to be treated as full citizens is a theme that runs strongly through Taylor *et al.* (2007), picking out powerfully all the overt and covert ways in which people with learning difficulties are denied the rights that others take for granted.

From good intentions to good practice

We want in what follows to consider ideas about translating commitment to participation into practice. The two managers given as examples for this chapter have a positive starting point. They are personally committed to greater service user participation. We note this here because the strong message from the literature from users is that there can be no other point of departure. For people interviewed in Beresford *et al.*'s (2011) research, for example, person-centred care was at heart about practice values, not practice techniques – the latter being approaches that you can choose to use selectively, the former being beliefs that inform all practice. This should not come as a surprise. Most people are able to sense when people are doing things which they believe in, and when they are turning on the official 'have a nice day' language of customer care. Bad faith has a certain smell.

What skills do people like Rupa and Sharon need to move from good faith to greater participation, and from there to improvements in service? Often this will be a substantial form of change, given that it asks questions about the nature of relationships and can be seen as a threat to established power bases. In caricature form, Figures 6.2 and 6.3 show what would happen if there were a fundamental shift of power.

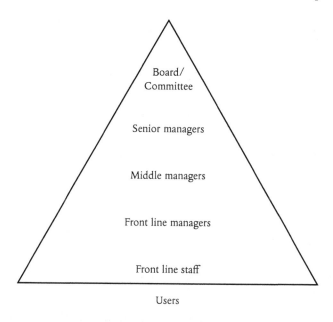

Figure 6.2: The conventional public service organization

In such organizations, accountability flows upwards, and users are outside the organization boundaries, recipients of, but not partners, in services. Power obviously resides within the hierarchy and increases as we go up the pyramid.

The radical shift model is fanciful, but it has the virtue of showing how dramatic changes might be in their impact on organizations. It also provides an interesting view of accountability. If accountability flows upwards, then the alternative model suggests that the board or committee is accountable to users. We do not want to suggest that this is the new 'ideal' organizational arrangement: boards, committees and senior managers have responsibilities to the wider public and to government, a reality seen starkly when budget cuts have been necessary. There is also a sense from the models that power is finite, whereas an era where collaboration and partnership become real might also be an era that challenges this zero sum view of power. Power might grow with users, but not because others have less of it.

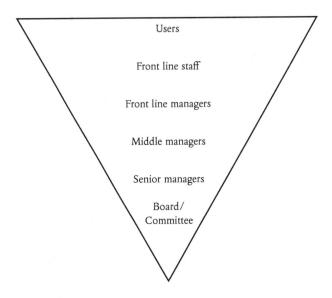

Figure 6.3: A radical shift in shape?

Making it happen – skilfully

Figures 6.2 and 6.3 indicate something of the direction of travel for Sharon and Rupa, and the amount of change that this might entail. They are engaged in change management, the subject of Chapter 3, in which we suggested an approach proposed by Smale (1996). In seeking change in this area, managers have the advantage of access to a wide range of guidance – unsurprisingly, given the profile of participation in policy terms over recent years. Sources that we have found useful include Baulcombe *et al.* (2001); Beresford *et al.* (2011); Branfield and Beresford (2006); Doel *et al.* (2007); Moriarty *et al.* (2007); Roulstone *et al.* (2006); and Simpson, House and Barkham (2002). In relation to the participation of young people, sources we have found useful are Wright *et al.* (2006) and Voice of the Child in Care (2004). There is considerable consistency and clarity in the headline messages from these guidance materials, which can be summarized as:

- hearts and minds
- clarity of purpose
- participation within organizations as well as outside
- attention to the small print.

The Social Care Institute for Excellence guides to participation (Wright *et al.* 2006 and Moriarty *et al.* 2007) stress the importance of a systems' approach, which fits with Smale's (1996) approach. The four elements that they argue need attention are culture, structure, practice and review. Key skills in using these approaches are those of analysis, engagement, communication, empathy, negotiation, problem-solving and evaluation. We use Smale's approach again here, but make use of ideas from the guidance sources cited above.

Thinking about participation using Smale's 'innovation trinity'

You were introduced to Smale's innovation trinity in Chapter 3, and here we apply the three elements to user participation.

Element 1: What needs to change? What needs to stay the same?

Clear thinking and communication is needed about purpose. What do we hope to achieve? Where does this come in Arnstein's ladder? What already happens that is consistent with the principles of participation?

Also Element 1: Who are the key people?

Will Rupa need to approach the families of residents? Has she used her negotiation skills with her manager and senior people in the company to gain support for this development? Are there advocacy/user-controlled groups locally which would be helpful partners? Are there 'hard to reach' users in Sharon's service and, if so, how will she seek their involvement? Has she spoken to the department's Children's Rights service? Would involvement from foster carers/residential workers be useful? Rupa might consider who in her staff group and among residents is likely to 'champion' the change, and who might resist it. Our two managers will then need to use their engagement skills to work with people and groups identified. They will also need to be aware of the details of the language that they use. Is the word 'participation' one that is familiar to their users, or will it come over as part of a manager's jargon? If people are comfortable with it, what do they mean by it?

Element 2: What is the nature of the change?

Would this change be fundamental or incremental? Is it about culture change? For whom? Staff? Service users? The wider organization?

Element 3: What is the context for the change?

Is it consistent with other changes? Will it be seen as yet another initiative that is here today and gone tomorrow? Are people already struggling to implement other changes? Are there other residential establishments in Rupa's company that have pursued better participation from whom she can learn? Is Sharon's department only interested in being seen to meet their performance indicators or does it see young people's involvement as important regardless of the type of measurement used (a question again of organizational culture)?

Running through all of this will be management style, particularly the extent to which front line staff are listened to and included. As Baulcombe *et al.* (2001, p.32) note, 'a "consultation culture" starts within the organization or work setting. Are staff consulted and involved?' Practice at an individual level also needs to be sound and is the starting point for wider participation, as Beresford (House of Commons Public Administration Select Committee 2008) argues: it would be an odd organization indeed that sought users' involvement in the running of services but denied them partnership in decision making about their own support needs.

Implementation

The next level of Smale's approach concerns negotiation and staff development. We think of it here as a process of implementation that needs continually to refer back to the questions raised earlier as more learning emerges. Having established clarity of purpose, identified key people and analysed the nature of the change towards greater participation, what are the key considerations in implementation? Lots of ideas come from the sources cited above, many of them practical. We are also grateful to Jackie Martin from De Montfort University's social work department for introducing us to the metaphor of 'space' when we talk of participation. Gaventa (2006) uses this in his analysis of citizen involvement. Here, let us think of participation as occupying a 'space'. Questions immediately suggest themselves from this, as in Box 6.3.

Box 6.3: Participation and 'space'

- Who owns the space?
- What are the symbols of ownership – physical layout, language, formality, timing, dress, place and so on?
- How big is it?
- How might its shape and size affect the willingness and ability of users to participate?

Rupa and Sharon might keep this metaphor of 'space' in mind as they get started on improving participation. It alerts us to some of the key skills needed:

- *Empathy*: What is it like for participants? What support/training do people (including staff) need to participate effectively in driving change? How can we arrange the 'space' to ensure it includes rather than excludes?

- *Planning skills*: When does real participation start? What payments, rewards and recognition are appropriate? How long is needed? What methods are likely to work? Guides for young people's participation, for example, stress the importance of variety and informality. Where is best to have meetings? How can we keep the momentum going – avoiding a drop off in interest after the initial excitement? How do we ensure proper diversity in representation? Are there adequate resources for the process?

- *Communication*: How do we ensure inclusion for all? Is our language accessible, both written and verbal? The language of performance indicators, key success criteria and impact assessment is unlikely to excite the residents whom Rupa wants to involve, but social work and social care has a language that can become so common that we forget it is an 'in-group' language.

- *Political skills*: Who do Rupa and Sharon need to influence? Who might be the 'change champions' whom Smale refers to? How will they deal with opposition? Are they politically able enough to bring any achievements and learning into the wider organization to help facilitate larger-scale change?

- *Negotiation skills*: Is participation based on negotiated aims? As implementation continues, unexpected things will happen, and managers need to be able to work positively with any conflict arising. In such negotiations, holding on to key values becomes important to avoid competitiveness taking over from collaboration.

- *Feedback skills*: People need information on how they are contributing; constructive feedback becomes an important but often undervalued skill for managers.

Developing user involvement includes developing the skills of managers, staff and service users to facilitate a co-productive approach. For Sharon, co-production entails implementing and enabling the involvement of children and young people in collective and individual decision-making processes. Learners, children and young people all have to be actively supported to develop key competencies. Wright *et al.* (2006, p.42) identify specific competencies (see Box 6.4) recommended for staff and service users to make any involvement meaningful.

Source: Wright et al. *2006 (reprinted with kind permission of Barnardo's)*

Box 6.4: Key competencies for staff and service users to make involvement meaningful

Competencies required by adults	Competencies required by children and young people
• Understanding what participation means and why is it important.	• Understanding what participation means and why is it important.
• Understanding the potential impact of participation (on children and young people and the organization).	• Understanding the potential impact of participation (on children and young people and the organization).

- Opportunity to explore attitudes towards participation and working in partnership with children and young people.

- Knowledge about different methods that can be used to involve children and young people.

- Communication techniques that enable the involvement of all children and young people.

- Responsiveness.

- Sensitivity to and awareness of the individual needs of children and young people.

- Opportunity to develop imaginative and creative techniques.

- Knowledge about how to work with children and young people safely and establish appropriate boundaries for their involvement.

- Opportunity to explore attitudes to participation and working in partnership with adults.

- Knowledge about different methods that can be used to involve children and young people.

- Opportunity to explore how they would like to be able to participate and what they would like to see changed.

- Team-building activities that enable the development of such skills as listening, being responsive to others, taking responsibility for specific roles, debating, communicating.

- Opportunity to develop confidence in expressing their own views.

- Skills in presenting own views and views of other children and young people.

- Skills and experience in relation to specific participation activities.

Review and evaluation

Implementation also needs review and evaluation skills, the last level of Smale's approach (1996). However, whilst everyone agrees on their importance, review and evaluation are vulnerable. They make demands on our time management skills, particularly our ability to pay attention to the important as well as to the urgent. Governments have been as guilty as anyone in failing to pay proper attention to this stage. 'Pilots' seem either to disappear or to continue as mainstream with hardly a pause for evaluation. We noted in Chapter 3 that evaluation is important because it helps to bring out learning: it can also lead, as Horwath and Morrison (2000) argue, to identifying reasons for celebration. 'Review' suggests an ongoing process, perhaps conversations on how things are that can lead to small changes. Evaluation, on the other hand, usually signals something more substantial, a stepping back from the process. Doel *et al.*'s work (2007) has many helpful suggestions on evaluation. They identify nine 'big questions' about evaluation:

1. Why bother?

2. What stops us?

3. What does making a difference mean?

4. When is it right to evaluate?

5. Who evaluates?

6. How should we do it?

7. What do we need?

8. How will conflict about impact be managed?

9. What will we do with the evaluation?

Box 6.5: 'On the Spot' – Why bother with evaluation?

The nine questions are quite a challenge to busy managers and might prove quite painful to face up to. However, one of the key themes of all texts on management, including this one, is that evaluation is fundamental to the search for improvements in any organization. Are you able to use the questions to assess current evaluation arrangements that you have in place? What improvements are needed to these arrangements? Are there other questions not listed that you have found are also of importance in thinking about evaluating user participation?

In considering these questions, you will have identified a number of reasons why managers may need to evaluate user involvement and the initiatives that seek to increase participation. There is certainly an ethical obligation to ensure that all interventions in social care practices are examined and reviewed regularly in terms of management accountability (Hafford-Letchfield 2010). Many aspects of evaluation form part of regulatory and statutory requirements. Organizations that have grown accustomed to such evaluation have sometimes been led into an approach to evaluation based on a need to *prove* – that we are OK, good, very good and so on. Here, the emphasis might profitably be on a commitment to *improve*. It is unlikely that managers will get everything right first time, so this process fits the broader process of seeking continuous improvement. Evaluation inevitably has a political dimension to it as politics and practices will have their sponsors and advocates with both positive and negative investment in the outcomes (Robson 2002). This indicates that evaluation is not an activity for managers sensitive to the criticism or controversy which may arise when evaluating directly with service users. The evaluating manager will need to have strong conflict resolution skills and diversity in perspective, using people management and good communication skills in order to get the best out of everyone involved (Hafford-Letchfield 2010). Whilst user involvement is right in itself, users do not want to waste their time engaged with activities that make no difference. Evaluation should therefore concern both the process and outcomes of participation.

Box 6.6: Service user commentary

'Being a service user is not the sum of my whole,
but a fraction in the equation that is life'

Involving service users in the planning, implementation and delivery of services is a leap forward in promoting recovery, well-being and stability amongst the client base. As 'experts by experience' our collaborative capacity and skill base can enhance existing services. Certain terminologies are barely within our grasp with respect of service user involvement experiences. Whilst at times many of us experience tokenism, I can guarantee that perseverance will pave the way for meaningful involvement activities, particularly those that lead to employment or higher education, such as in my own case. Participation, collaboration, partnership working have all been experienced in my involvement journey over a period of time with meaningful outcomes which have improved the quality of my life.

Service user involvement has the capacity to also fulfil the esteem needs of some service users. For example, I feel motivated to be involved in social work and social care service as they help me to have some of my needs met, such as physiological, safety, social, esteem and self-actualization. I agree with Maslow on those ones (1943) whose hierarchy of needs recognized that meeting the basic needs for comfort and safety are not enough and that self-esteem is a normal human desire in which we all want to be accepted and valued by others. The esteem needs, for example, can be addressed by involvement opportunities which enable a sense of belonging, recognition, attention, social status, accomplishment and self-respect. These contribute towards an upward spiral in the service user's hierarchy of needs. In my experience as both service user and provider of services to service users – best practice is hard to maintain, but good practice has longevity!

Christine Khisa

We conclude with some thoughts about balancing what managers want or need to achieve with how service users themselves identify with managers' attempts to engage them in participation, and issues to consider from their perspective, particularly if you find them difficult to engage or start to feel frustrated in your attempts. There are alternative analyses. Simmons (2009) asserts that having a 'voice' goes beyond the confines of choice, allowing people to express things such as the depth of feeling on an issue or a sense of membership, solidarity and support.

As we saw earlier when discussing the young people Sharon wishes to engage, some users have greater levels of personal resources such as time, money, education, skills and confidence which generally support how they exercise their voice and presumably choice. There are, however, two further sets of factors which are termed by Simmons (2009) as 'subjective' and 'objective'. Subjective factors concern how people see themselves as public service users, and objective factors concern how connected people feel to the service itself. Simmons's research (2009) looks at different 'subjective' and 'objective' aspects of user involvement, for example by analysing where users feel able to have a say and make a difference, combined with a sense of connection or disconnection with the service itself. The way users identify with services may be individual or collective. For example, users might feel that individually they can have a say and make a difference. However, they might feel disconnected from the goals and aims of the service. These users could be seen as apathetic and not caring enough about the service to engage with it further. Simmons suggests (2009) that this may be attributed to lack of understanding about the significance of the choices available, and building relations through a wider programme of public engagement might create more connected 'consumers'. For example, Sharon might undertake some broader activities drawing in those associated with young people and young people themselves in the community. If, however, users see themselves as members of a collective, this may lead to being seen positively as being able to have a say and make a difference even if users do not feel a strong sense of connection to the service itself. The users' role here is limited to 'delegation' by giving their allegiance and deference to those who have political or authority status, such as senior managers. They accept that these people will arbitrate between the different demands on their collective resources in the public interest and the user will be able to 'vote' for this periodically. Users' influence is therefore one step removed from the actual provision of services but they trust in those with a higher authority. Rupa may encounter this in her residential home where some issues are passed up to the head office in the company. At higher levels of discourse, users may argue for modes of coordination that promote individualistic values such as personalization and autonomy and be connected collectively to the coordination and co-production of the service. The users' role here is to involve themselves in deliberative and participative processes that are specific to the service or service issues. Collective action therefore takes place in a range of processes that includes user groups, peer advocacy and campaigns. Users have an expectation of responsiveness to their demands which are derived through collective processes and expressed through collective channels to demonstrate solidarity. At higher levels of actualization, users may argue for services to be organized in ways that promote mutual values such as equality, solidarity and association.

Chapter summary

This chapter has illustrated that commitment to participation should be visible in the principles held and the practices demonstrated by managers. These can be built in to your everyday practice where user involvement is reflected within planning, service delivery, how services are resourced, day-to-day communication and activities designed to improve services. Commitment to participation should extend to staff development so that both you and the staff you manage have the opportunity to develop the skills and attitudes to engage effectively with service users as part of your everyday work. Some organizational hierarchies may make participation a challenge for front line managers and it is important in these situations to avoid tokenism, where participation doesn't really fit with the short-term results orientation of the organization. Even in these circumstances, Pine and Healy (2007) assert that it is never efficient to reach a decision that no one will implement or commit to because no one has consulted or involved those being affected. This includes both users and staff and reinforces some of the principles visited in Chapter 3 on managing change. Even with medium-range goals, participation can often strengthen outcomes of services and regular evaluation of your initiatives should help to demonstrate progress. Wright *et al.* (2006, p.13) recommend a whole systems approach to effective service user participation, incorporating four interacting elements. First, the importance of culture where the ethos of an organization demonstrates a commitment to participation; second, that organization's infrastructure, which needs to be able to facilitate any planning, development and resourcing of participation; third, that the methods of working in direct practice utilize the skills and knowledge of staff to enable service users to become involved; and fourth, the evidence that the organization produces, through its monitoring and evaluation systems, of any changes affected by participation and the ways in which these are reviewed. There are also different degrees of involvement such as those illustrated in the Arnstein (1969) and Simmons (2009) models. Improvement for Rupa and Sharon will start with their personal commitment and be brought about through their skilful and resilient translation of this into a process that recognizes users as citizens with a right to a voice. In improving participation they will be making an invaluable contribution. They will have lessons to teach us all.

Action checklist

1. Reflect on the true meaning of user participation and involvement in your organization and get support from people above and below you before implementing any initiatives.

2. Train staff and service users in skills to increase their confidence in working in social work and social care hierarchies.

Chapter 7

Skilful Negotiation and Conflict Management
What about the Tricky Bits?

The major difference between you and other people is that you know what you are thinking and feeling, whereas other people know only what you look like and how you are behaving. This fundamental difference between you and everyone else makes your behaviour extremely important.
Honey 2001

Developing themes from the chapter on managing change, we will look more closely at the skills required in situations involving conflict. This chapter draws mainly on principles from relationship based theories and psychological approaches. We will be utilizing some of the work done by psychoanalytic system theorists on the skilful use of questioning techniques and positioning theory (Huffington *et al.* 2004; Tomm 1988) and how this might be integrated with some of the documented research on the use of political skills, not often valued in care environments (Leslie and Canwell 2010). This chapter will encourage managers to think about both informal and formal approaches to managing conflict and the use of negotiation skills in working with different parties.

Putting conflict in context

It is inevitable that conflict will arise within a manager's role and, whilst it is tempting to avoid confrontation or situations in which conflict is likely, it is poor management practice not to attempt to resolve issues. Conflict resolution is connected to the ways in which managers use their power. Unresolved conflict can become a destructive force within the team or organization. Managers may get things done through their use of authority, manipulation, politicking or influence, and motivate people by using overt forms of power (Lawler and Bilson 2010). Equally these methods may be more subtle and complex and vary over time. As we have seen in previous chapters, creating a climate where all people are treated with respect and feel listened to will greatly reduce the potential for conflict.

The importance of how power is perceived and utilized within social work and social care organizations cannot be overemphasized. This is particularly evident when negotiating between the rhetoric and realities of practice where there is a frequent mismatch between expectations and available resources, and a simultaneous drive to improve service and demonstrate value for money. For example, studies of how people become managers (Bryans and Mavin 2003; Hafford-Letchfield and Bourn 2011) highlight the emotional stress involved as one transitions into management roles. Whilst there has been a continuous stream of helpful insights drawn from the critical literature on management (Clarke 2004; Hafford-Letchfield *et al.* 2008; Lawler and Bilson 2010), very few studies (Aronson and Smith 2009; Healy 2002; Maddock 1999) have focused on the actual experiences of those who manage social and community services. These have highlighted how managers might distance themselves from managerialist practices or develop resistance to find more participatory opportunities for staff and service users. For example, in a qualitative study of Canadian women managers, Aronson and Smith (2009) discerned two broad strategies deployed by managers to develop the critical consciousness of those they managed. The first strategy should incorporate significant effort to expand the entitlements to service users increasingly excluded from public transport. The second should incorporate efforts to politicize and expand the scope of practice in their organizations by sustaining advocacy in their work; embedding sophisticated knowledge of institutional politics and enormous skill in using language to expand, deepen practice and develop the critical consciousness of those they managed: 'as long as you'd speak about 'policy development', 'planning'. I mean who could say no to that right? So we played up to that stuff (Aronson and Smith 2009, p.14).

Combining such political skills with interpersonal ones may enable us to work more effectively within the social contexts of social work and social care organizations, which are essentially dynamic environments for both organizing and structuring social relations (Hearn and Parkin 2001) and may be underpinned by assumptions on the way one is assumed to manage or be managed (Hafford-Letchfield 2011). The National Social Work Taskforce (DCSF 2009) highlighted working conditions on the front line of services in which poor communication and antagonistic relations between staff and managers served to work against the capacity of managers to lead and manage services. Managers themselves experienced unmanageable workloads and expressed unmet needs for adequate support and continuing professional development. However, knowledge of deeper power relations can help, as the image that we live in a world shaped by forces over which we have little control is both overwhelming and leads to complacency and feelings of futility (Morgan 1993). As stated at the beginning of this chapter, failure to negotiate can affect the very survival of an organization as well as contribute to secondary stress disorders that can occur in the helping professions such as 'compassion fatigue', 'secondary traumatic stresses', 'vicarious trauma' and 'burnout' (Figley 1995). Burnout is characterized by work-related emotional distress with emotional exhaustion, depersonalization and lack of satisfaction and can have physical manifestations. Giving attention to these problems not only helps to combat current issues in social care, such as retention but, as Thomas and Otis (2010) note, identifying and being proactive in those factors that contribute to satisfaction can generate positive feelings in the helping profession.

Understanding sources of conflict

When dealing with conflict it is important to understand its source and how to manage confrontations. Common causes of conflict in social work and social care arise from:

- poorly managed change where there is a lot of uncertainty and stress

- excessive, arbitrary or inappropriate use of power

- situations where inadequate resources may be allocated to meet service users'/carers' needs

- inequalities, discrimination and harassment and lack of attention to diversity and rights.

Ola is an experienced manager in a Learning Disability service. He manages an integrated team who are very dynamic and have won several awards for innovative projects. The team have just relocated to share premises with the Children with Disabilities team. This was partly driven by efficiency savings and partly to promote stronger partnerships around service users' experiences of transition from children's to adult services, and is the first stage for both services in restructuring and working under one 'Disability Independent Living Support Services' umbrella.

Ola has been asked to mentor Josie, the new deputy manager in the Children with Disabilities team. This is going very well, Ola finds Josie very intuitive and creative although she has limited experience of learning disabilities. It is agreed informally with their overall manager that Josie should gain some experience in the Learning Disability services. Ols's team appear very supportive. All goes well and six months later during the second stage of restructuring, Ola gains promotion to Disability Services Manager and at the same time Josie is promoted to a new role as manager of the integrated service.

Shortly after this, things start to deteriorate in the team. There is a backlog of work building up, a number of complaints from carers about quality issues and a higher level of sickness absence. Hassan, the senior practitioner, has told Ola that he is going to put in a formal grievance to Ola's manager stating he has been discriminated against in the reallocation of posts arising in the restructuring. His non-cooperation with Josie's new role has caused split loyalties within the new service and Ola starts to dread going to work as there is an uncomfortable atmosphere. His manager Ted has told him to 'get a grip on the team' and 'show leadership skills' as this is part of his new role. His manager has also appointed Katie, a colleague, to investigate the grievance and mediate if possible.

Conflict covers a whole spectrum of behaviour from mild disagreement or difference of opinion through a range of work issues, to extreme mutual loathing between team members. Whilst the conflict in the above scenario may appear to have appeared out of the blue, this may have been brewing over time. Typically, a seemingly non-controversial issue can trigger a more explicit manifestation of conflict, such as in this case, a formal grievance. You may already recognize some of the potential issues after reading Chapter 4 on recruitment and selection skills. Typical sources of conflict may involve:

- differences between individuals or sub-groups in work direction or approach

- the presence or formation of cliques or exclusive groups

- a desire to perform well as a team but where not everyone is pulling their weight

- confusion or resentment of allocated roles

- unfair treatment, cultural differences and poor management of equality issues

- differences in perceived effort expended by individual members

- personality clashes.

It is important to reiterate here that conflict isn't necessarily always a destructive force and some have argued that it can actually be constructive (Tillet and French 2006). For example, the very differences that cause conflict can also provide a rich source for generating new ideas and open the mind to new possibilities. Conflict can also allow you to refine your team's defence of its ideas against criticism and generate a passion for retaliation allied to the key issues, for example where ethics, values and equalities are at stake. What is important, however, is not to allow disputes at work to become personal. Fighting passionately should be allied with the key issues and not with the people involved. The concept of positioning in any situation is characterized by a process of relationship building where interaction with others allows their personal narratives on the issues to emerge (Mason 1993).

Pritchard (2000) highlights the importance of training staff to manage conflict, which she says is not just something that you identify but needs to be actively worked with by someone with the necessary skills. Therefore Ola should not just be expected to 'get on with it' as Ted has asserted. Ola will need to be given support and facilitated in developing the skills for tackling the situation in his service. Pritchard's suggestions for good practice involve:

- spending quality time with the different parties

- avoiding being pressurized into rushing assessment of conflict to suit the needs of the organization

- identifying 'conflict' as an area to work on

- setting goals to resolve conflict

- if appropriate, identifying other workers or agencies who may be able to help with negotiation and mediation

- recording what methods or resources are being used to resolve conflict.

It would be easy for the situation in Ola's team to escalate, with an unsatisfactorily resolved grievance going forward towards a legal resolution such as an employment tribunal. Before going on to look at skills required for resolving conflict in these types of scenarios we are going to step back and focus on some of the intrapersonal skills managers can draw on which prevent or contribute to a more dynamic environment so that conflict is perceived as a more creative force.

Intrapersonal skills in dealing with conflict

When we talk about intrapersonal skills, we are referring to your own ability to reflect and monitor your own progress, thoughts and feelings, strengths and weaknesses as you go about your management tasks. Being sensitive to our own feelings enables us to have better interpersonal skills. These skills are those which are often referred to in management as the people skills, the way we communicate with others for example through active listening, body language and the way we behave and carry ourselves in relation to others.

Empathy is consistently considered as an important factor in the development and maintenance of effective relationships. Human empathy involves the capacity to take on the perspective of the other person/s. Managers who have stronger empathic skills have strong self-awareness, executive control and emotional regulation skills, which are aspects of emotional intelligence. Thomas and Otis (2010) talk about achieving a state of 'mindfulness' which involves the capacity to pay attention to what is happening in the moment. Here the manager doesn't focus on creating elaborate mental stories about their experience where they are more likely to react to negative thoughts or become emotional. Ola could easily become very defensive about the atmosphere developing in his team and use his new authority to stamp out areas of discontent. However, he could also take time to reflect on the experience without judgement or avoidance. For example, by not jumping into response mode as demanded by his manager – 'get a grip' on it – Ola could appraise the situation 'from a de-centred, distanced perspective, which allows for more reflective, intentional action and less impulsive, automatic reactivity' (Thomas and Otis 2010, p.85).

These ideas are drawn from the application of psychoanalytic concepts from systems theory which enable us to think in more depth about some of the unconscious processes and communication in groups and organizations and provide a rich and powerful model to apply when difficulties arise (Armstrong 2004). Being alert to the emotional undertow of team life can be a powerful source of information for managers in enlarging their understanding, reviewing people's performance, foreseeing challenges and opportunities and guiding management decisions and action. Ola will need to give attention first to his intrapersonal skills or abilities with the aim of reducing the risk of further conflict with Hassan; his longer term aim will be to increase his own and the team's resilience to conflict and to improve the work satisfaction of all the people involved. The capacity to work in a way that attends to resistance and negative processes in organizations, combined with systemic approaches, has been described as 'working below the surface' (Huffington *et al.* 2004). Research by Thomas and Otis (2010) demonstrated that mindfulness and emotional separation are significantly associated with the ability to express compassion and experience satisfaction. Developing these abilities will also help to avoid burnout and to achieve emotional separation that can be significantly associated with compassion fatigue. Their findings suggest that increased emphasis on the intentional management of internal emotional states may be as important for managers and practitioners as for service users. Professional education or in-house training programmes should consider how best to teach such skills. Gallagher (2010) also proposes the use of a SWOT (Strengths, Weaknesses, Opportunities, Threats) analysis to analyse one's own emotional state. For example, you can use this to speculate on the potential impact if you behaved differently in work and personal situations. Using SWOT in this way enables you to identify your own emotional strengths and weaknesses, and by explicitly labelling these you can make some decisions about how you might maximize your use of emotions or utilize them better in different work situations. In summary, a great deal can be learned from the individual's emotional and perceived irrational responses to the organization and by moving away from conceptualizing these as a source of disturbance in team or organizational functioning.

Using communicative techniques which embrace 'curiosity'

Hypothesizing

We are going to explore the concepts of curiosity, hypothesizing and neutrality which some systemic theorists have suggested might be adopted as a set of practices and actions that can be transferred into different professional contexts with a positive effect. We more often talk about 'hypothesizing' in association with research. In this context it is described as a process of generating explanations by looking for connections among what you observe, data you collect, and personal experience with prior knowledge. Hypothesizing is based on transient suppositions rather than fixed beliefs and on circular ideas rather than lineal ones. Within leadership and management practice, hypothesizing can be adopted as both an approach (a way of thinking) and a technique (a way of doing). As an approach hypothesizing invites us to take up multiple positions in relation to what is going on in the organization or team. In relation to the case study above this may help us to appreciate the complexity, for example by hypothesizing about where Hassan might be coming from, his story about his position in the organization so far and how the alleged discrimination he is experiencing relates to his overall experience and knowledge of the organization. As a technique, hypothesizing invites us to name the connections we make, and to create possible explanations for the situations in which people find themselves. Cecchin (1987) suggests that being curious helps us to continue looking for different descriptions and explanations for everyday issues that occur, even when they are difficult to imagine. In becoming curious, we are creating the context for hypothesizing. Another way of thinking about curiosity is through the analogy of a butterfly which settles momentarily. Hypothesizing replicates this transience by moving through different ideas. Hypothesizing then is useful, not because it enables us to capture reality at that moment in time, but because it is a means of generating more ideas and flexibility in our thinking. The nature of hypothesizing prevents us from becoming fixed on one explanation or way of thinking with the consequence of being unable to find alternatives. These latter habits are more likely to reduce our chances of resolving conflict. Ola's manager Ted could, for example, initiate some hypothesizing in his supervision with Ola and perhaps with Katie, to consider the issues from different perspectives and how the current situation might be tackled. Imagine the scenario if Ted makes himself available to staff in the service over a period of time to facilitate them expressing the issues they feel they are facing and particularly in finding out what Hassan wants to achieve. He may find that issues in relation to the restructuring are preventing progress, or that insufficient work has been done to integrate the two teams now working under one service umbrella, given that this has been a period of intense change. Some of these strategies hark back to those we looked at in Chapter 3. No doubt one could generate a number of other hypotheses regarding the above scenario, many of which may differ given the different and personal positions we tend to take up.

It is important to develop the habit of reflecting on the way that you and others negotiate. The increasing amount of time spent in negotiations creates a considerable opportunity to learn from the skills used or even the mistakes made. The stereotype of the effective negotiator is the person who drives a very hard bargain. However, the key to effective negotiation is in developing procedural and process skills so that the framework and the way in which you conduct negotiations is such that you are able to achieve what is potentially attainable (Rees and Porter 1996). Thinking about how often we express curiosity and how easily we take up a position is a skill all managers and practitioner should consider developing. Undertaking the listening exercise in Box 7.1 might help to develop your ideas about what curiosity and positioning theory has to offer. This could be done the next time you attend a meeting between several people, or a meeting between someone in authority with someone they manage or supervise. You could also listen to everyday conversations between professionals and service users.

Box 7.1: 'On the Spot' – Listening exercise

1. Make some notes on the overall direction of the conversation – did you note any specific examples of curiosity?

2. If curiosity was expressed, what influence did this have on the direction of the discussion; did it make any difference for example in the power relationships or cooperation between those involved?

3. If there was an absence of curiosity, what hypothesis were you able to formulate about why the person did not adopt a curious stance?

By embracing the systemic concepts and practices of hypothesizing, you can enhance your own potential for curiosity and with it, greater neutrality. Given that we are likely to come across conflict regularly in our roles as managers, this is another useful skill to develop. It is usual to try to frame hypotheses in tentative language which captures their transient nature. When talking about neutrality, the same ideas apply, where professionals retain a lighter touch. Some of these ideas featured in the discussion in Chapter 6 where we examined the approach to co-production and the importance of being non-judgemental and open to the influence of others. A feature of these tendencies is to adopt more tentative language in our exchange with people, for example, by using terms such as: 'I wonder if'; 'I am curious about', etc. Another is attempting to make connections between different bits of information that offer some explanation for the current situation and being cautious about settling on one which may not be any more true or false than others, but just useful or not. In creating hypotheses in this way we avoid a cause-and-effect approach as well as avoiding the uses of deficit language which can affect the esteem of those we are talking to. In social work and social care most people are doing the best they can, often in difficult and challenging circumstances. If we, as professionals, can hold on to an appreciative view, we are part way to helping people move from deficit language and action to the language of ability and resourceful action.

Using 'systemic questioning' to enhance skills in negotiating and managing conflict

Tomm (1988) developed a framework in which he distinguished four major groups of questions that we might use to guide our decision making and which can also be used to generate more therapeutic conversations. Therapeutic questioning is derived from the Milan systemic approach (Campbell and Draper 1985) and seeks to promote consensual agreement. This is a useful skill for managers in demanding work situations as it demonstrates commitment towards being helpful in resolving any difficulties and promotes a more participatory approach. Whilst this might appear obvious, a frequent critique of managerialism in social work and social care is the tendency for more directive or didactic conversations. Tomm (1988) asserts that the linguistic form taken in your contribution towards conversations can have an important effect on the nature and direction of the evolving conversation. For example, asking questions rather than making statements may create more active dialogues, convey a commitment to listening and foster autonomy in colleagues' own decision making, which ultimately frees up your own resources and time as we saw in Chapters 2 and 5. Whether done consciously or not, the purpose of actively 'asking' arises from the conceptual posture of strategizing. Actively asking and listening can guide your moment to moment decision making during a discussion with the intention of reaching a consensus (Tomm 1988). Tomm's four major groups of questions are used in this chapter to inform skills in negotiation and conflict management by relating to our use of our self within our management roles. Asking pertinent and awakening questions of those we are working with enhances the other person's own capacity. The four types of questioning that Tomm described in his work are what he calls lineal, circular, strategic and reflexive questions.

LINEAL QUESTIONS

These are basic questions: Who did what? Where? When? and Why? Most conversations begin with at least some lineal questions. The conceptual posture of lineal hypothesizing contributes to the content issues in a conversation and provides a subject focus for generating these lineal questions. So, thinking about the dispute above, this is likely to take up a lot of time and prove very emotional and draining for those involved. Most conversations at work begin with lineal questioning, perhaps to determine the issues, but can tend to convey a judgemental attitude and often provoke defensiveness in those on the receiving end. For example, Ted may have said to Ola: 'Why can't you get a grip on the situation? After all, don't you realize that your role involves keeping the lid on the staff issues to make sure they don't affect the quality of the services.' Alternatively, Ted might have asked: 'What exactly has Hassan complained about?'

CIRCULAR QUESTIONS

The intent behind these types of questions, on the other hand, is predominantly exploratory. You take on the role of an explorer, and set out to make a new discovery. The guiding presuppositions are interactional and systemic. Circular questions assume that everything is somehow connected and questions are formulated to facilitate connections between persons, objects, actions, perceptions, ideas, feelings, events, beliefs, contexts and so on, in recurrent cycles. Examples might be: What are you worried about? What happens when you are feeling anxious? What can stop you feeling anxious? Circular questions tend to be neutral and accepting and characterized by a general curiosity about how events are connected rather than a need to get to the root of the problem or its underlying cause. They involve skills in maintaining a conceptual posture in hypothesizing which come across as more neutral and accepting, such as: 'I was curious about why you (Hassan) are not happy with the current situation and when this all started? I was wondering what might have happened from your point of view to make you feel so angry with the management here.'

STRATEGIC QUESTIONS

The intent behind these questions is predominantly corrective, assuming that you need to be more instructive or directive. On the basis of hypotheses formulated about the dynamics of the situation, the manager might conclude that something is wrong and so uses strategic questions to get people to change or think and behave in ways that might improve the situation. Examples might be: 'When are you going to get that report written?' or 'Why don't you talk to Hassan about the issue and get it sorted?' Asking strategic questions enables the manager to impose their views on somebody in the belief that a more directive or confrontational approach can help a situation which appears to be 'stuck'. There is always a danger of disrupting relationships when asking strategic questions, however. Sometimes a directive or confrontational mode is required to move someone who feels stuck although this can run the risk of disrupting your own relationships temporarily: 'Ola, given that you have described a lot of resentments in your management relationship with your colleague Hassan, why haven't you set aside a time to discuss these directly with him?'

REFLEXIVE QUESTIONS

The intent behind these questions is predominantly facilitative where the manager acts as a guide or coach encouraging others to mobilize their own problem-solving activities and resources. A reflexive question might be: 'Let's imagine Hassan is feeling angry and defensive right now because he wasn't successful in his application for the job – what would happen if you just acknowledged this and said how sorry you were for his disappointment?' Reflexive questions are more neutral and are usually influenced by your own emotional posture in asking what might make a difference to the situation being discussed. They are also predominantly facilitative and assume the autonomy of those they are directed at. These make reflexive questions highly relevant for professional practice in social work and social care. Reflexive questions are designed to trigger people to reflect upon the implications of their current perceptions and actions and to consider new options. They require well-developed skills in assuming a position of neutrality. In all of these different types of questions there needs to be attention to emotional tone and posture.

The application of questioning techniques in social work and social care management

A number of studies on the quality of supervision in social work and social care have described supervision being driven by a target-driven culture of organizations, with limited opportunities for critical reflection on the complex and often ambiguous nature of the work (Bourn and Hafford-Letchfield 2011). Social workers who receive a more therapeutic style of supervision (Baginsky *et al.* 2010) have reported how it contributed to their own well-being and ability to cope with stress. More bureaucratic and 'tick-box' models of supervision are felt to be counter-productive to development alongside other workload pressures which prevent some workers from taking up other professional development and post-qualifying training opportunities. These all contribute to situations of conflict and dysfunction in services such as Ola's. In considering hypothesizing, circularity and neutrality we can begin to understand the 'knowing whilst not knowing' approach to those we work with and this will help us to be more participatory and empowering leaders. As professionals in different contexts we bring with us different expertise that will most certainly influence our approach with those we work with. However, if we can introduce the notion of neutrality and curiosity into our repertoire we might find that we can hold on to our expertise but be continually open to other ways of seeing the world. If, as professionals, we can move between ideas in this way, we are more likely to be able to help others see their problems/issues differently and that is sure to make life easier!

Negotiation skills

Not all situations can be resolved by paying attention to the above issues alone, as these skills are related to increasing one's objectivity. They point to the importance of developing your intrapersonal skills so that your influence can be beneficial in both informal and more formal situations. Policies and procedures provide further safeguards in ensuring that the rights of staff and service users are adhered to and upheld where there is a dispute. These are particularly important in relation to promoting equality and ensuring that people's employment rights are upheld. Within the social care context, commercial and working arrangements have to be renegotiated as services change and develop, particularly within changing political and socio-economic circumstances or in relation to operational matters. These require political skills alongside detailed knowledge of legislation and policy. Informally negotiation may involve being sensitive to the needs of staff and meeting the expectations of other managers, as referred to above. In more formal situations there should always be opportunities for interaction so that at the end of any negotiation all the parties involved are satisfied that an appropriate deal has been struck and that there is a 'win–win' situation. In any negotiation there should be an emphasis on the common ground, with a willingness both to relate to the concerns of the other side and to compromise where necessary. Negotiation is a complex process, during which the concerns of both sides should be identified, usually through questioning. The terms and conditions of any deal struck should be arranged and agreed.

Negotiating and the bargaining process

Walton and McKersie (1965) distinguished between distributive and integrative bargaining. Distributive bargaining refers to a situation where one party can only gain at the expense of the other whereas integrative bargaining provides potential to increase what can be distributed. One example might be in determining social workers' productivity. For example, in the above scenario, staff may be offered additional payments for taking on extra roles such as an Approved Mental Health Practitioner or a Best Interest Assessor within the new Disability service. Negotiation also requires preparation in advance. Different variables such as the people involved, the objectives and structure of the negotiating process, have to be taken into account and considered. It should also be remembered that in most instances you will still need to be in a relationship with the other party at the end of the negotiation and this is a good incentive for avoiding bad feelings. Scott *et al.* (2008) discuss how the way individuals behave in a negotiation will depend on how much they want to meet their own needs and how much they want to meet the other party's needs. For example, the process of working through Hassan's grievance will need to consider how this takes account of repairing future working relationships, no matter what the outcome. If Hassan has been a loyal and productive member of the team, Ola will not want him to leave. Box 7.2 gives a short guide to the different areas involved in negotiating which can act as a quick reference guide.

Box 7.2: Negotiation – Some common areas to consider in the process

Stage 1: Preparation – questions to ask

- Who are the people involved, what do you know about them?
- What are their concerns and motivations?
- What will different parties want?
- Are you able to meet these?
- What are your own objectives?
- What will happen if the negotiation fails?
- What would be your bottom line?
- What do you have to trade and what concessions may be possible?
- How will you structure the negotiation and the order of events or activities?
- How will you present yourself?
- Is your approach in keeping with what is expected from you in your role?
- What power do you/other people have?

Stage 2: The process

- How are you going to conduct the negotiation?

- Think about tactics.

- Anticipate all the variables that could be on the negotiating table.

- Do you have the power of reward, agreement or punishment?

- Aim high as you can always lower your expectations.

- There is a human tendency to want to win when negotiating but this can increase the conflict involved and there are consequences for managers who go in too hard.

- Your interpersonal skills and behaviour can make a lot of difference to the outcome.

- Develop rapport and show respect to the parties involved.

- Be prepared to make concessions, especially those that don't cost much.

Negotiating techniques

- Start off with a neutral subject, to build rapport and atmosphere.

- State repeatedly the value of what you are offering.

- Present a clear explanation, summarize frequently and take notes.

- Constraints and variables are often interchangeable.

- Ask questions to clarify points.

- Use silence and don't be afraid of silence.

- Read between the lines – what do they really want? – and be aware of any non-verbal language.

- It might be easier to limit to one representative or have someone to help you so you can feel supported and to exchange notes privately at intervals during the process.

- Do not get hung up on deadlines, and keep thinking.

- Maintain neutrality and objectivity.

- Do not make a final offer until everything is on the table.

- Leave the other party feeling good.

- Be aware of your own emotions and those of others.

(based on Forsyth 1991)

Arbitration

- If unable to reach agreement, use arbitration. Appoint somebody neutral and ensure that both sides respect and trust the arbitrator.

- Abide by any decisions made during arbitration.

- Ensure that where there is direct conflict, or if you are acting as an arbitrator yourself, you maintain a harmonious atmosphere.

- Find a resolution that allows for realistic decisions to be made and for things to move forward.

- Do not allow personal feelings or relationships to influence decision making.

Managing uncertainties without being curious, hypothesizing or tentative, and without negotiating the personal dynamics between colleagues or between managers and their staff, can lead to very high tension. This will usually be played out in accusations, hostility and recriminations. There has been an increased demand for skills in conflict resolution and mediation interventions within social work and social care organizations. This calls for training in mediation skills for managers to reflect growing incidents of conflicts in the day-to-day work, and allegations of bullying and harassment leading to grievances. Mediation is seen as an informal intervention to resolve the situation rather than resorting to formal disciplinary procedures. It lends itself to social work and social care as it seeks to empower the people involved. The use of mediation to resolve a grievance or situation of conflict can be seen as a positive step forward in that it requires a process of inquiry and negotiating a resolution rather than investigation and blame (Hoyle 2004). This shouldn't stop us from asking about the root causes. Hoyle (2004) highlights the significance of changing from more traditional, hierarchical structures where people in a position of authority were clearly distinguished. We have now moved much more towards flatter hierarchies and increased competition between care services. This has given rise to greater pressure on people to improve their individual performance, take responsibility for their own personal development and to manage themselves. As relationships between managers and employees changes this should also enable individuals to feel more autonomous and able to challenge. It requires managers, however, to have the capacity to be able to tolerate being challenged and questioned as well as to deal with the inevitable tensions and conflict situations that arise.

A lack of management containment of conflict situations, where attempts to prevent escalation have failed, can be addressed through mediation if a neutral third party is involved. Ted has appointed Katie in the scenario above, who will begin to investigate the cause of Hassan's grievance with a view to problem-solving. As Katie moves through these processes she will need to keep accurate records of the process and she will be asking Ola for his own record of how he has responded to the situation so far. Any records should be kept in accordance with the Data Protection Act 1998, bearing in mind that this gives employees the right to access any personal information relevant to them.

ACAS (Advisory, Conciliation and Arbitration Service) (ACAS 2009), an organization which aims to improve organizations and working life through better employment relations, gives the following advice:

- Both employers and employees should raise and deal with issues promptly and should not unreasonably delay meetings, decisions or confirmation of those decisions.

- Employers and employees should act consistently and deal with issues informally where possible.

- Always carry out any necessary investigations to establish the facts and inform employees of their findings and give them an opportunity to put their case in response before making any further decisions.

- Agree a way forward with realistic and reasonable targets that the employee can meet.

- Keep brief notes and use these to review. Always give the employee a copy so they are clear about what has been agreed and the consequences for failing to achieve change.

- Allow employees to be accompanied at any formal disciplinary or grievance meeting.

- Allow and provide process for appeals against any formal decision made.

- Learn from issues and adjust any policies or practices to avoid future conflict.

Chapter summary

Policies and procedures in social work and social care organizations provide a strong basis from which managers can work to avoid bias and deal fairly with the many different situations that can arise. However, procedures are just one means of managing conflict and this chapter has addressed some of the interpersonal skills that managers need to manage situations which may be challenging. Importantly, managers can act as a catalyst to encourage parties involved in any dispute to reflect on their roles in the situation and to help them develop strategies to overcome the difficulties. Conflict often escalates over a period of time, so managers needs to be constantly observant for signs of potential breakdown in relationships, including their own day-to-day relationships with those they are working with. We have given a lot of emphasis in this chapter to the importance of developing good communication skills and awareness of the emotional undertow in organizations. Signs may include a change in the atmosphere or non-specific complaints about an individual's attitude or behaviour, or an increase in absence when individuals are allocated to work together. As we saw in Chapter 3 on change, uncertainty and ambiguity can be heightened during change processes, in particular, around the power and authority that can be exercised by those in leadership roles. According to Hoyle (2004) external forces create the need for people to make an effort to relate better to each other. This is increasingly so because of requirements in social work and social care for more corporate working, greater involvement of staff in decision making and increased collaboration. At the same time pressure on individual performance and the experience of personal vulnerability can militate against changes, as we saw in the case study above. Managers therefore need to keep their eye on relationships between others so that individuals and their teams can cope with and contain the tensions associated with continually changing roles, accountabilities and contexts.

Action checklist

1. Make good use of policies and procedures to set standards and as a reference point where there are disputes or problems in the team.

2. Work on your interpersonal skills and adopt a curiosity and hypothesizing approach to resolving problems.

3. Seek help from people in your organization to consult and mediate where problems are escalating.

Chapter 8

Effective Mentoring and Coaching

Skills in Developing Others

The behaviours that define learning and the behaviours that define being productive are one and the same. Learning is not something that requires time out from being engaged in productive activity.
Zuboff 1988, p.395

If you think education is expensive, try ignorance.
Attributed to Derek Bok

Introduction

Social work and social care rarely if ever involve minimal skill in predictable environments. The more typical mixture is complexity of task and volatility of environment. Social work and social care managers face constant demands not just from the immediate operational context but also the wider environment. Government policy refers to a commitment to 'modernization', 'transformation' and the like. Managers quickly discover, however, that one government's modernization is the next government's focus for reform. As we saw in Chapter 4 in relation to recruitment and retention, the profile of the social work and social care workforce remains complex and offers a range of challenges through changing patterns of migration, demography, policy directions and socio-economic circumstances.

Pre-set solutions are seldom available so that managers and practitioners constantly need to monitor the impact of their behaviour on others and to fine-tune their approach; they need to learn as they go.

They are learning through doing, as Zuboff suggests in the quote above. Not all learning, however, is 'good' learning, and this creates problems for managers who are committed to their service getting better: how to harness individual learning for the collective good? We want to explore this area of management responsibility in this chapter, a responsibility that can get buried in the busy-ness of work. If it is ignored too much, adaption of Bok's quote should also remind us of the consequences: if you think development is expensive, try stagnation. In exploring learning in the workplace we are investigating a subject that has increasingly interested researchers in recent years (Lee *et al.* 2004). This is hardly surprising, given that for most people, most of what they learn *about* work is learned *at* work. We have in mind two managerial activities: supporting individual learning through mentoring, and developing a team climate in which learning becomes part of work and is shared. Done effectively, these give a considerable return on the investment of time.

Mentoring in social work and social care

We begin with mentoring. The word 'mentee' to describe the person being mentored is awkward, but we use it because it is the word most often used, and seems more appropriate than the other commonly used word, 'protégé'. All texts will tell you that the word 'mentoring' is derived from Greek mythology, the Odyssey, in which Mentor was trusted to be the wise advisor to Telemachus. Mentoring is a relatively new word, but people through the ages have mentored others:

- The phrase 'showing the ropes' comes from an old sailing tradition in which experienced sailors would teach newcomers how to tie the ropes safely. Here, we would have found mentoring and coaching both being used.

- The development of crafts saw the use of a similar model, with apprentices working alongside older workers to learn the craft.

- 'Sitting with Nellie' (inducting new workers by putting them next to an experienced person) was a similar example in the cotton industry, again combined with coaching.

- The guru–disciple relationship in Hinduism has aspects of mentoring within it.

Many people reading about mentoring come to realize that they have had relationships which have had at least some of the characteristics of what we now call mentoring. It has been popular in the management literature since the 1980s, first in the US (with focus mostly on careers) and then becoming more prominent in UK literature (more focused on development). We now find it across a wide range of circumstances: for senior executives, disaffected young people, newly qualified teachers, nurses and social workers and care leavers. It came into the 'official' language of social work and social care through the Central Council for Education and Training in Social Work in the 1990s.

In search of a definition

We have noted some of the many circumstances in which mentoring is used. Surveying the mentoring scene, Hay (1995) summarized some of the words and phrases used to describe what happens in mentoring, and we show these in Box 8.1.

Box 8.1: What happens in mentoring?

- Showing the ropes
- Passing on knowledge and skills
- Being a sounding board
- Helping put learning into practice
- Being a role model
- Career counselling
- Coaching
- Guiding

Source: Hay 1995

Finding a definition which travels across all contexts is difficult. However, we have chosen one that is often cited and which makes sense in relation to our current interests from Clutterbuck and Megginson (1995, p.13): 'Off-line help by one person to another in making significant transitions in knowledge, work or thinking.'

'Off-line' here means outside the traditional line management process. Our view is that managers can be mentors if we accept that effective social work and social care management includes attention to individual development. There is an overlap with supervision, particularly in relation to skills. However, we want to stress that there is a different dynamic at work when a manager is acting as a mentor compared to those meetings labelled supervision. When we engage in mentoring we 'park' accountability (unless something untoward comes up, in which case the mentoring session will need to move into a different sort of conversation) and focus on development and learning. There are, however, obvious overlaps between mentoring, supervision, counselling, coaching and appraisal: differences are sometimes ones of emphasis, and more about context and purpose than skills.

In reality, few mentors will apply a 'pure' model, and close observation of the process would sometimes reveal a blurring of boundaries, especially between mentoring and coaching. A number of books on the subject recognize this by referring in their titles to both coaching and mentoring (see, e.g. Brockbank and McGill 2006; Foster-Turner 2006; Megginson and Clutterbuck 2005; Parsloe and Wray 2000). Hafford-Letchfield *et al.* (2008) have shown how a blend of the two can be a powerful developmental tool.

Box 8.2: 'On the Spot' – My career and significant people

What we call things is perhaps less important than how they work and their value. This is so with mentoring. Think back over your career. Are you able to identify people who have been particularly helpful to you, giving you time to reflect on work and yourself? Was this because of how they behaved with you, the circumstances at the time, their individual qualities – or a mixture of all of these and others? In your current post, are there people who might look to you as an important person, beyond any formal relationship you have with them? How do you respond to this?

Thinking about your experience should have alerted you to the very individual nature of mentoring. There is also, of course, an organizational context for it. Much of the mentoring literature takes the world of business as its main source of reference and caution is needed in trying to transfer lessons to social work and social care. The mentoring role in social work and social care has often been accompanied by assessment and is nearly always time-bounded: examples being practice assessors/educators in social work qualification, supervisor-mentors for newly qualified social workers, mentor-assessors in post-qualifying programmes, and the arrangements for induction in social care. These are thus often 'hybrid' models, and carry little in their remit about general career development or providing openings for mentees into promotional opportunities; activities that are often discussed in mentoring literature, particularly books based on the American model.

Whatever model/mixture of models is used in mentoring, what emerge as critical to success are:

- developing rapport – the relationship
- clarity of purpose – scope and goals.

Each needs the other. Clarity of purpose without rapport limits development to the superficial, and rapport without clarity of purpose looks more like friendship than mentoring. Low rapport and low clarity means just 'going through the motions' (Clutterbuck and Megginson 2005, p.18).

The manager as mentor

The pressures of management in social work and social care mean that it might be desirable but not realistic to think of managers routinely as mentors to their staff. Our approach in this chapter is that mentoring becomes a powerful tool for development in particular circumstances. Let us take three people:

> Alake, has just started working as a care assistant in a residential home for older people. She has done various jobs, none of them proving satisfying. She heard of 'care work' from a friend. Alake thought of her mother looking after her granddad, and became interested; at least she would be doing something useful for people. Rupa, the assistant manager, has high hopes for Alake, who came across at interview as enthusiastic and personable.
>
> Dipak, is starting his social work career in a children's services social work team. With a placement in a Sure Start

Centre giving valuable experience of working with children and parents, he now needs to transfer this to a statutory social work setting and to the responsibilities of a qualified social worker. Gerry, his manager, looks forward to working with him on the Newly Qualified Social Workers' (NQSW) programme; he likes the idea of working with someone starting his or her career.

Sally, has moved from a care manager post in a local authority after five years to a specialist post in a voluntary sector agency, with responsibility for developing a new service for older people with mental health problems. Shilpa is her manager and keen to make best use of Sally's experience and expertise.

Here we have three people at different points in their career, all facing new responsibilities, all with skills and knowledge gained from work and elsewhere, all in a *transition* during which much learning will happen at many levels.

Dipak's transition is from student to professional practitioner with professional responsibilities – and anxieties. Alake's transition is from outsider to insider: her thoughts will be about whether this is a career for her. Sally's transition is about context and culture: from the statutory to the voluntary sector, from working with individuals to developing services.

Mentoring with Dipak and Alake is likely to be blended with coaching (and some assessment) because of the point in their careers, whereas with Sally it might involve little coaching, focusing mostly on the transfer of her experience and expertise into a different context; indeed, her recruitment will have been in part to do with what she will bring to the organization. Common to all, however, will be the overall context: working in social work/social care, with the associated set of values about anti-discriminatory and anti-oppressive practice, promoting independence and respect for people. As you read on, you may wish to have in mind anyone similar in your team, either past or present. We want to look at how mentoring might be a valuable process with people in such transitional situations.

The relationship develops and power shifts

No mentoring will succeed if the tone of the relationship is not right. As with any relationship we should expect it to develop and change over time. Most texts on mentoring acknowledge this, and see it as having a number of stages, anywhere between three and seven. Clutterbuck (1998, p.95), for example, identifies five stages:

1. rapport-building

2. direction setting

3. progress-making

4. maturation

5. close-down.

Morton-Cooper and Palmer (2000) have reduced these phases to three:

1. initiation

2. working phase

3. termination.

There are many variations on the number of stages and what they are called (see, e.g. Brockbank and McGill 2006; Megginson *et al.* 2006), but all have at heart this sense of travelling from getting to know each other, through agreements on goals, reflection on and work towards goals, and ending. One last thought about these stages: whilst it is important that the mentee's development is the central concern, it is our experience that successful learning through mentoring is two-way: something which Phillipson (1998, p.16) found. Her enjoyment is clear when she writes about the aspects of mentoring she likes, including: 'waking up in the morning and realising I'll be...mentoring for part of the day – a treat' and 'learning from and with each other – so much better than one head'. It is important to acknowledge this mutuality at an early stage.

For our three people – Alake, Dipak and Sally – their circumstances will make the process slightly different. For Alake and Dipak, some of the purpose is 'given' by the national standards for induction and for newly qualified social workers, and some of the manager's work will be to do with helping them achieve these standards. However, there is a danger that the paperwork of competence takes over, leaving little space for the personal reflection that supports professional growth; the mentoring process becomes shallow when reduced to ticking boxes for official purposes. Chalfont and Hafford-Letchfield (2010, p.40) note that staff learning is not just about achieving competence at the instrumental level. For example, importance has been given to the provision of space for reflection in an evaluation of the Newly Qualified Social Worker programme, reporting that 'Regular, structured reflective supervision was the feature of the programme most highly appreciated by the NQSWs' (Carpenter *et al.* 2010, p.63).

Alake, Dipak and Sally arrive at their new jobs with varying mixtures of excitement and anxiety. This will influence the early part of a mentoring relationship, which is likely to be the one in which power is most obviously with the mentor. In the literature on mentoring, power is usually seen as shared, but Rumsey's (1995) research into mentoring in post-qualifying social work education provides a framework for understanding why power only becomes shared over time. Her analysis is summarized in Box 8.3. Early on, Dipak will be keen to check with his manager, Gerry, on procedures, Alake will be anxious to do things in accordance with accepted standards, and Sally will need Shilpa's support in understanding how much freedom she has to innovate. As time goes by, however, these managers should expect less checking up activity and more independent decision making during the second and third stages of Rumsey's framework. Indeed, if people are 'stuck' in dependency it becomes important to explore why this should be so. In the latter stages, the newcomers, more confident and organizationally street-wise, move from being recipients to beginning to be contributors. It is here that the benefits of mentoring to service users and the organization become most obvious. Not only does mentoring support individual development, it also provides space for new viewpoints and perspectives that bring fresh energies to teams and act as a positive challenge to current orthodoxies.

Table 8.1: Power shifts with the growth of confidence

Stage	Mentee characteristics	Environment required
1	Dependence, learning needs yet to be conceptualized	Structured environment, positive feedback, task-focused
2	Moving between dependence and independence	Less structure, need for emotional support
3	Increased confidence, with some conditional dependence on mentor	More sharing, with professional and personal challenge
4	Personal control and insight	Working alongside worker, helping knowledge to become wisdom

Source: Ramsey 1995

What we want to stress here is that this power shift is a sign of healthy progress in a mentoring relationship. As the mentee relationship enters the second and third stages it also moves into the working phase, and we turn to this now.

The working phase: GROW

What happens in this stage of mentoring will depend on the goals agreed earlier. This is the space, away from busy practice, where the bigger picture can be addressed, and where the mentee has the opportunity to look at things in different ways. The key management skills required are reflection and action planning. GROW (Whitmore 2009) is a model that is common in the literature on coaching and mentoring and it can be applied both to individual sessions and to groups of sessions.

G = Goal, what is it you want to achieve for yourself?

R = Reality, what is the current situation?

O = Options, what is it possible to do?

W = Wrap-up, what are you going to do?

(www.mentoringforchange.co.uk)

There are variations between writers about the word associated with O and W – Outcomes and Options for the O for example, and Will, Wrap-up or Way Forward for the W. Here we have chosen Options and Wrap-up. The model is valuable in two ways. It not only supports reflection within the mentoring process, but also provides a very simple structure – described by some as a map…and maps are valuable when you get lost. We suggest how GROW might apply in Box 8.4, using newly qualified social worker Dipak as an example. Over time, it is important that you develop a repertoire of techniques to bring life to the process, and Megginson and Clutterbuck have gathered together a wide range of these (Megginson and Clutterbuck 2005; 2009). These form a valuable resource though, as the authors acknowledge, the best techniques are often those that the mentor him or herself has devised. They also warn against the misuse of techniques, which can 'lead to helping-by-numbers, where the user does not have the knowledge or skill to use the technique appropriately' (Megginson and Clutterbuck 2005, p.7). Foster-Turner (2006) has similar words of caution about techniques becoming ends, not means. As you look at our suggestions in Box 8.3, therefore, think about what techniques you might prefer.

As he starts his career after qualifying, Dipak wants to develop his confidence in applying the law and local policies and procedures. He wants to work on his time management. He has a particular passion for working with children where parental mental health is a problem. He has told his manager, Dan, that he really just wants to become 'the best practitioner I can'. He has therefore identified some 'Goals'.

Endings: 'parting is such sweet sorrow'

In many of the mentoring relationships written about in the literature, the process is long term and sometimes grows into friendships. Here we have looked at time-limited arrangements, but where the working relationship will continue. Whatever the context, endings are best built into beginnings. Any initial mentoring agreement should thus include timescales, with an awareness that you might need to be flexible. There are also times in the middle of mentoring arrangements, when you and the mentee might revisit timescales and draw up a shared plan about what still needs to be completed. Endings benefit from some simple ritual – perhaps the exchange of thank you cards, or perhaps doing something different that symbolizes ending this phase of the relationship. Often a looking back on the process is useful and always a planning ('what next?') activity helps.

Skills, values and self-awareness in mentoring

We have suggested in outline what a mentoring process might look like, arguing that GROW can be used both for individual sessions and the overall process. With Alake, her mentor manager will also need to do some coaching, for example demonstrating some practices to her, given her newness in the job. With Sally, Shilpa might follow a more straightforward mentoring model, and it is likely that power will more quickly be shared between them. What does all this mean for managers who want to succeed in mentoring individuals through transitional periods? Morton-Cooper and Palmer (2000) argue that effective mentors share the following:

- *Competence,* arising from knowledge and experience, and in interpersonal skills

- *Confidence* in allowing the mentee to develop within their own terms, in leadership, and in dealing with other people's problems and recognizing their achievements.

- *Commitment* to people and their development.

Box 8.3: The mentor manager's responses – Some techniques

Goals

Gerry will need to help Dipak move towards more specificity about learning needs. He might therefore use the SMART (Specific, Measurable, Achievable, Relevant and Timed) model of objective-setting. He might, however, leave Dipak's 'best practitioner' goal in its general form, so that Dipak can unpack for himself what this means.

Open questions are very useful here, for example: 'How will you know when you have got there?'

Reality

Dipak and Gerry need to examine the current position. Gerry might suggest that Dipak does a SWOT (Strengths, Weaknesses, Opportunities, Threats) analysis, which is often useful for people who are anxious and forget the positives that they bring to their work. He might also encourage Dipak to consider feelings through open questions: how does it feel to be in this team? What is it like no longer to be a student?

Options

Dipak now needs to think about ways of tackling his goals. Gerry needs to have an understanding of the various ways in which people can develop their skills and knowledge. He might ask Dipak 'How might you achieve this?' whilst having in mind a range of ways of learning to prompt Dipak as appropriate.

He might suggest using a cost-benefit analysis for each option. Keeping a diary to capture his views on best practice fits here. Brief bullet points about situations where he feels he or a colleague have practised to a high standard would help Dipak develop a clearer picture of what he means by best practice. It would also provide a focus for reflection between mentoring meetings.

Wrap

This last step ensures that a move from intention to action is more likely. Whilst motivation is important (which is why some writers call this step 'Will'), also important is helping Dipak to plan in the light of the pressures of work. Questions such as 'What do you plan as your first step?' and 'What might get in the way?' are helpful to get Dipak actively thinking about making it happen. Gerry might at some point suggest that he uses a simple form of project planning.

In stark contrast, Darling (1986, pp.29–30) warns of 'toxic mentors':

- *Avoiders*, who do not respond to mentees' messages.

- *Dumpers*, who expose mentees to the 'deep end' inappropriately and without support.

- *Blockers*, who refuse requests, withhold information or mentor too closely.

- *Destroyers/criticizers*, whose feedback is designed to put down rather than facilitate learning.

How do we avoid becoming toxic, instead becoming the sort of mentor suggested by Morton-Cooper and Palmer's analysis? Table 8.2 covers key areas.

Table 8.2: The making and shaping of effective mentors in social work and social care

Skills in	Values	Self-awareness	Knowledge
Relationship-building *Demonstrating empathy* *Motivating* *Open questioning and active listening* *Reflecting and helping the mentee reflect* *Constructive feedback*	A belief in change and development A belief in sharing power and responsibility A commitment to learning	How controlling am I? Am I happy that there is more than one way of doing most things? Am I open to learning from the mentee?	Knowledge is important, but not in a teacher–student way

Mentoring, learning and the team

We see mentoring as a cost-effective activity for social work and social care managers that marries up individual development and improving service quality. In our experience of mentoring new workers we have found that the process is enriched when it happens in a supportive team atmosphere. Indeed, it might be the case that mentoring in an unsupportive environment ends up being of very limited value. We want therefore to think about this broader context for learning: the team. As a manager, you have an opportunity that you probably lacked before: an opportunity to develop the team as a place for learning. Integral to this is an approach to leadership which we have referred to elsewhere, namely 'distributed': a style in which the leader recognizes that leadership can be displayed by others in the work group. Individuals are viewed as resourceful learners, and teams as learning resources. If work and learning are to coexist constructively, you need to work on developing the team as a learning resource for itself and others through sharing power and responsibility.

Types of workplaces

To help you think about this approach to team learning, let us consider evidence about the workplace, which shows that some workplaces are more conducive to collective learning than others. There are several reasons for this:

- *The broader organizational culture*, which at each extreme can either encourage learning or block it. The organization where blame is quickly allocated is not one where people feel safe enough to seek and share learning from experience.

- *The team context* – collaborative teams are greater than the sum of the parts, and make mutual learning possible. Kitchen discussions in which ideas are shared help shape future thinking only when people are willing to work together.

- *The approach of line managers*. Those who view learning as important find time to promote it despite other pressures. Those who practise empowerment find more ways to share responsibility for learning throughout teams than those who manage through command and control.

- *The attitudes of individuals*, with some more willing to share ideas than others.

These, in varying combinations, create a distinctive climate for learning in teams. Stern and Sommerlad (1999) analysed the work–learning relationship in workplaces and found, broadly speaking, three sorts of possibilities:

1. Work and learning are separated: training happens, but away from the workplace.

2. Learning is planned and organized in the workplace.

3. Learning and work are seen as inseparable. Here we find more emphasis on and attention to 'informal' learning and learning through experience, as well as continued attention to more formal learning. These workplaces have a commitment to continuous learning, and learning and performance are acknowledged as closely connected.

Learning organizations

In social work and social care, where the work is subject to such changing circumstances, the idea of work and learning as inseparable is attractive; it is seldom enough to wait for the next training session. This comes across strongly in the literature on the 'learning organization', a management concept that has caught the imagination of consultants and academics since it was first popularized by Senge in *The Fifth Discipline* (1990). A search for books on www.amazon.co.uk in August 2011 gave nearly 4000 results for 'learning organization'. A popular definition sees the learning organization as 'an organization that facilitates the learning of all its members and continuously transforms itself' (Pedler, Burgoyne and Boydell 1991, p.1). Many view the idea as aspirational: in sociological terms as an 'ideal type' which will not be found in reality but which provides criteria against which organizations can measure themselves if they want to maximize learning. An important headline argument in all of this is that the learning organization is an effective organization. Honey (1991) helps to cut through some of the many thousands of words written about the concept by identifying some assumptions behind it such as:

*   learning is a 'good thing'

*   learning is better planned than left to chance

*   learning is a continuous process

*   collective learning lasts longer than individual learning

*   some behaviours (such as blaming, deference, covering up) conflict with learning organization principles.

Most of the literature on learning organizations is set at the level of the whole organization, but we believe that the practices that flow from these assumptions are valuable at team level: indeed, one of the five 'disciplines' for learning organizations suggested by Senge is 'team learning'. We use the word 'climate' to capture the sense of a particular atmosphere in teams, rather than 'culture'. Whereas front line managers may have limited influence in the short term on the overall culture of their organizations, they do have influence over what happens in their teams – the climate in which people work (Chalfont and Hafford-Letchfield 2010; Holt and Lawler 2005). Thus a team's climate might be receptive to learning even if there are larger organizational barriers.

Implications for managers

There are compelling reasons in social work and social care for keeping learning alive in teams. Environments characterized by high levels of sharing and openness to new ideas and learning through experience are usually livelier. Motivation tends to be higher in these teams. Service quality improves. In all of this the manager is critical. So what are the important lessons from this for managers who want to encourage the development of learning as an integral part of practice? We now want to explore this.

First, it raises questions about values in and for management. A learning environment cannot be developed when managers behave in a way that disempowers staff, because it requires staff to feel comfortable in taking responsibility. A management style which on the one hand primarily controls staff activity and on the other asks people to share responsibility for their and others' learning sends out contradictory messages. Managers need therefore to be aware of the impact of their behaviour and the gap between this and their stated beliefs. Second, it needs teams which function well. Positive teamworking means that the team can become its own learning resource. Not that this is without problems. The evidence on 'groupthink' (Janis 1972) should be a warning to all managers and team members about the dangers of cohesion blurring into collusion: a commitment to the group's way of thinking that precludes healthy conflict or alternative viewpoints. For the climate to be receptive to learning, the team therefore needs to be open to challenge from within and from outside.

Mentoring can also promote interprofessional learning for managers themselves. Hafford-Letchfield and Chick (2006) evaluated a mentoring initiative that they developed over three years across a range of partner organizations and which involved a primary and acute healthcare trust, two local authorities, a local university, a voluntary sector organization and two independent consultants. These came together to form a work-based learning partnership and an 'interagency mentoring scheme', which encouraged and recognized participants as the 'creators' and 'users' of their own learning. Premised on beliefs and evidence suggesting that partnering across the organizations at different levels can contribute towards quality care, the inter-agency mentoring scheme that Hafford-Letchfield and Chick (2006) developed attempted to mirror relationships developing between the partner organizations at personal and organizational levels to deliver local services. By focusing on commonalities and difference in values and approaches between managers from different organizations and agencies towards developing their staff, the scheme coordinators worked with key human resource personnel in local agencies to see if there was potential to share staff development tasks with other disciplines. Hafford-Letchfield and Chick concluded that managers from different organizations or professional cultures in the sector may not always see their own interests as coinciding, and using mentoring in the inter-agency context demonstrated the benefits of the individual nature of support and provision of learning that a scheme like this can offer. Their scheme encouraged a framework which allowed managers to link personal and individual learning with organizational practice alongside themes or areas of work-based skill development that preoccupied them at key periods in their development. Given the emphasis on integrated working, this scheme recognized that some of the management skills required are interdependent and changeable (Hafford-Letchfield and Chick 2006). As government policy and initiatives require a more joined-up culture, using mentoring across different disciplines or agencies can provide managers with the opportunity to gain insight and awareness of the different organizational backgrounds of the mentor/mentee, as well as the transferability of skills and knowledge that highlights our common purpose.

Making it happen: using our skills

Managers with a commitment to team learning need also to have the skills to make it happen. Key skills are:

- *Team building.* Team learning is frustrated by an atmosphere in which people do not trust each other or where the emphasis is on individual working practices.

- *Encouraging participation.* This approach needs all to take responsibility.

- *Working positively with diversity.* If Handy is right in arguing that 'teams are collections of differences' (1990, p.125), then managers need to harness these differences, not repress them. Team learning will bring multiple perspectives to the surface which will enrich the service.

- *Information sharing.* Many managers now suffer information overload because of the developments in technology. Managers need to be able to use technology to enhance team learning instead of drowning it.

- *Motivating.* Some individuals find collaboration easier than others, and some find presenting ideas in a group difficult. Quiet voices might well be important voices, though, and managers need to help each person make their contribution.

Making it happen: some methods

We conclude this chapter by sharing a few ideas from our own experience:

- case discussions (what you call it will vary depending on the location of your work)

- asking each person to develop a particular area of interest on behalf of the team, and reporting back on this when appropriate

- co-working

- buddying more experienced with less experienced workers

- a regular development slot in team meetings – or meetings divided between 'business' meetings and development meetings

- shadowing

- team members visiting similar teams and reporting back on good ideas

- shared team knowledge folders, whether in hard copy or computer-based form

- celebration of successes

- a commitment to having students on placement – from a variety of courses.

These are just some of the ideas about putting team learning into practice and you may have plenty of your own.

Chapter summary

Our experience is that life for social work and social care managers is busy. Not occasionally but relentlessly. This puts real pressure on managers to find time for the important as well as the urgent, and a casualty in this can be sustained attention to learning at work. As a colleague once reflected, those most in need of development time seem often to be those with least time for it. We have tried in this chapter to remind you of its importance along with some ideas on making it work. Behind all of this is an argument worth restating: time spent on development is an investment for the future – for the individual, for the organization and for users of the service.

Action checklist

1. Make time for learning in your team which has 'an invest to save' component where retention and succession planning of staff is concerned.

2. Value work-based learning which provides rich opportunities for staff development.

3. Take advantage of your own opportunities for mentoring, particularly with peers from other disciplines where available.

Appendix

Auditing and Assessing Your Own Management Skills Using the Multi-Source Feedback Tool

Please refer to the last section of Chapter 1 for an explanation of this tool.

There are various ways in which it can be used:

- as a one-off audit to identify a benchmark in order to plan and develop your management skills

- on a more regular basis to sharpen and maintain attention to your practice

- when preparing for or transitioning to a new management role

- as a quality assurance tool with your team

- in preparation for appraisal and succession planning.

The tool is based on a Likert scale. Adding up the scores is approximate only and designed to provide:

- an analysis of your strengths and areas for development

- a ranking of the relative importance of each skill to your own work environment and role in your organization

- identification of any discordance through seeking feedback from relevant others (peers/manager/staff/service users) using a multi-source feedback style

- help in creating a list of priorities of areas for your own skills development and personal focus.

Five proformas make up this multi-source feedback tool:

- *Multi-source feedback tool 1*: Proforma for gaining feedback from staff that you manage.

- *Multi-source feedback tool 2*: Proforma for gaining feedback from your line manager.

- *Multi-source feedback tool 3*: Proforma for gaining feedback from your peers.

- *Multi-source feedback tool 4*: Proforma for gaining feedback from the multi-disciplinary team.

- *Multi-source feedback tool 5*: Proforma for gaining feedback from service users and carers.

Finally, there is a proforma to record your individual Learning and Development Plan.

All proformas are downloadable from www.jkp.com/catalogue/book/9781849052061/resources.

Good luck!

✓

Multi-source feedback tool 1: Proforma for gaining feedback from staff that you manage

Dear colleague,

Thank you for agreeing to participate in contributing to feedback on my management skills. This questionnaire has been designed to help me obtain planned feedback from you on my current skills and complements similar questionnaires that have been completed by others, for example, myself, my own line manager, peers and service users [delete as appropriate]. This will enable me to get more rounded feedback from different perspectives. I would be very grateful if you could take the time to complete this questionnaire in the most honest and constructive way possible. The time suggested to complete it is around 30 minutes. The information given in this questionnaire will be kept anonymous and confidential. The information you give will not be discussed with you after you have completed the questionnaire and will be used for my own purposes only and shared with my learning mentor.

Please rate your perception and experience of my management skills in the following areas by circling the most appropriate response.

	Skills demonstrated in your management of the bigger picture	Seldom	Sometimes	Quite often	Often	Always
1	S/he is deeply motivated to make improvements to the services s/he is responsible for	1	2	3	4	5
2	S/he recognizes the effect of emotions on relationships at work	1	2	3	4	5
3	S/he recognizes the personal impact on group dynamics	1	2	3	4	5
4	S/he facilitates the development of a shared community vision that is influenced by the views of diverse stakeholders	1	2	3	4	5
5	S/he sells the organization's strategy to others in a way that facilitates their buy-in to any action plans and the next steps	1	2	3	4	5
6	S/he establishes clear standards for staff and service users and has transparent ways of monitoring these	1	2	3	4	5
7	S/he promotes a culture in the workplace that improves quality	1	2	3	4	5
8	S/he actively discourage a risk-aversive environment	1	2	3	4	5
9	S/he is committed to managing the diverse interest groups and powerbases in the organization so as to lead the service more effectively	1	2	3	4	5
10	S/he promotes diversity and equality in the team in a way that goes beyond legislation	1	2	3	4	5
11	S/he creates a climate where people can think creatively about practice, systems and processes	1	2	3	4	5

	Skills demonstrated in managing staff	Seldom	Sometimes	Quite often	Often	Always
12	S/he encourages people to be innovative and actively support their ideas	1	2	3	4	5
13	S/he contributes to developing and testing new ways of working	1	2	3	4	5
14	S/he actively involve service users and carers meaningfully in proposed changes to services	1	2	3	4	5
15	S/he builds communication processes that make it safe for people to say what is really on their minds	1	2	3	4	5
16	During the first stage of creating collaborative relationships, s/he takes time to establish common ground among all stakeholders	1	2	3	4	5
17	S/he demonstrates their own beliefs that trust is the foundation for successful collaboration for change	1	2	3	4	5
18	S/he invests adequate time within their busy schedule for 'people' development	1	2	3	4	5
19	S/he creates opportunities for people to learn new skills including leadership skills	1	2	3	4	5
20	S/he contributes to the well-being and productivity of staff in everyday practice	1	2	3	4	5
21	S/he feels confident in their knowledge and use of health and safety legislation and procedures	1	2	3	4	5
22	The information systems developed in the team allow them to identify service users' feedback on the service they receive	1	2	3	4	5
23	S/he is committed to developing people from diverse backgrounds	1	2	3	4	5
24	S/he have developed and regularly use clear measures that tell them about the quality of the service	1	2	3	4	5

25	S/he asks people they manage to regularly define their expectations and act on these	1	2	3	4	5
26	S/he communicates and agrees with staff and service users on how to work together to improve the service	1	2	3	4	5
27	S/he allocates work effectively and fairly among members of the team	1	2	3	4	5
28	S/he has the strength and resolve to hold others to account for agreed targets and take action where required	1	2	3	4	5
29	S/he assesses staff performance through the regular use of observation and feedback	1	2	3	4	5
30	Recruitment and selection to positions in the team seem fair and transparent	1	2	3	4	5
31	S/he is clear about the plans for us to work in partnerships with others to develop, take forward and evaluation direction, policies and strategies in our service area	1	2	3	4	5
32	S/he helps me to understand how our service contributes to the overall performance of the organization	1	2	3	4	5

	Embedded management values and principles	Seldom	Sometimes	Quite often	Often	Always
33	S/he is seen as someone who inspires staff to get the most out of their skills and knowledge	1	2	3	4	5
34	S/he consistently challenges discrimination and harassment in the work place	1	2	3	4	5
35	S/he values the people they manage and actively encourage their potential	1	2	3	4	5
36	S/he is in touch with service users' issues and has a means of establishing and understanding their needs	1	2	3	4	5

37	S/he provides an environment in which staff can develop reflective skills and practice	1	2	3	4	5
38	S/he takes responsibility for helping me with my professional development and the development of others you manage	1	2	3	4	5
39	S/he has developed plans to address specific issues of discrimination within our service area	1	2	3	4	5

Thank you very much for taking the time to complete this – the information will be kept confidential and used for my own self-development purposes only.

Proforma for assessing feedback from your staff team members/supervisees – to be completed by the manager

Use the boxes below to add up the scores that the staff you have managed have given you for each area. The notes below give an indication of how you have done and the degree of action required in response.

Skills demonstrated in your management of the bigger picture	Seldom	Sometimes	Quite often	Often	Always
Questions 1–11: Insert the total scored under each question and add them up					
Total					

Score 1–15: Needs attention
Score 16–35: Scope for improvement
Score 36–55: Very good feedback

Skills demonstrated in managing staff	Seldom	Sometimes	Quite often	Often	Always
Questions 12–32: Insert the total scored under each question and add them up					
Total					

Score 1–30: Needs attention
Score 31–79: Scope for improvement
Score 80–100: Very good feedback

Embedded management values and principles	Seldom	Sometimes	Quite often	Often	Always
Questions 33–39: Insert the total scored under each question and add them up					
Total					

Score 1–10: Needs attention
Score 11–22: Scope for improvement
Score 23–35: Very good feedback

Now complete the next two sections:

1. Your thoughts and reflections on feedback from your staff and/ or supervisees. Which areas came out strongest? Which areas did you not score so well in? How is this similar or different to the way in which you perceive yourself? Were there any surprises?

2. Record your conclusions here – how does this fit with or differ from other sources of feedback you have received?

✓

Multi-source feedback tool 2: Proforma for gaining feedback from your line manager

Dear line manager,

Thank you for agreeing to participate in contributing to feedback on my management skills. This questionnaire has been designed to help me obtain planned feedback from you on my current skills and complements similar questionnaires that have been completed by others, for example, myself, the staff that I manage, my peers and service users [delete as appropriate]. This will enable me to get more rounded feedback from different perspectives. I would be very grateful if you could take the time to complete this questionnaire in the most honest and constructive way possible. The time suggested to complete it is around 60 minutes.

The information given in this questionnaire will be kept anonymous and confidential. The information you give will not be discussed with you after you have completed the questionnaire and will be used for my own purposes only and shared with my learning mentor.

	Managing self and personal skills	Seldom	Sometimes	Quite often	Often	Always
1	S/he examines his/her personal resources, such as skills and knowledge, and regularly reviews the time needed to undertake his/her work role effectively	1	2	3	4	5
2	S/he regularly reviews his/her work performance against agreed objectives	1	2	3	4	5
3	S/he makes sure his/her practice fits into the overall vision and objectives of the organization	1	2	3	4	5
4	S/he reflects upon and develops her/his own practice using supervision and support systems	1	2	3	4	5
5	S/he regularly clarifies what values are driving her/him in terms of her/his own career aspirations and career vision	1	2	3	4	5
7	S/he can describe her/his strengths realistically	1	2	3	4	5
8	S/he can describe her/his weaknesses realistically	1	2	3	4	5
9	S/he is deeply motivated to make improvements to the services s/he is responsible for	1	2	3	4	5
10	S/he recognizes her/his personal impact on group dynamics	1	2	3	4	5

Your score: add up all the numbers scored under the above frequency. Write the number here: _____

Score 50–41: Excellent

Score 40–28: Strong

Score 27–16: Opportunities for development

Score 15–1: Important to develop further

Line manager's comments:

What do you think are her/his strengths in managing her/his own skills and reflective practice?

What do you think are the most important areas for improvement in the manager's ability to manage her/himself?

What is the relative importance of working on this area to her/his work at the moment – give any examples.

	Providing direction to others	Seldom	Sometimes	Quite often	Often	Always
1	S/he has a clear and up-to-date picture of the strategic environment in which this organization operates	1	2	3	4	5
2	S/he has a clear idea of resources available internally and externally to the organization that can help her/him achieve her/his goals	1	2	3	4	5
3	S/he actively contributes to strategies to guide the work of the service/organization	1	2	3	4	5
4	S/he facilitates the development of a shared community vision that is influenced by the views of diverse stakeholders	1	2	3	4	5
5	S/he sells the organization's strategy to others in a way that facilitates their buy-in to any action plans and the next steps	1	2	3	4	5
6	S/he establishes clear standards for staff and service users and has transparent ways of monitoring these	1	2	3	4	5
7	S/he promotes a culture that improves quality	1	2	3	4	5
8	S/he actively discourages a risk-aversive environment	1	2	3	4	5
9	S/he is committed to managing the diverse interest groups and powerbases in her/his organization so as to lead her/his service more effectively	1	2	3	4	5
10	S/he promotes diversity and equality in her/his team in a way that goes beyond legislation	1	2	3	4	5

Your score: add up all the numbers scored under behaviour frequency.
Write the number here: _____

Score 50–41: Excellent   Score 40–28: Strong
Score 27–16: Opportunities for   Score 15–1: Important to develop
development   further

Line manager's comments:
What do you think are your manager's strengths as a leader on a strategic level?
What do you think are the most important areas for improvement in providing clear direction to others?
What is the relative importance of working on this area to her/his work at the moment – give any examples.

	Facilitating change	Seldom	Sometimes	Quite often	Often	Always
1	S/he creates a climate where people can think creatively about practice, systems and processes	1	2	3	4	5
2	S/he encourages people to be innovative and actively supports their ideas	1	2	3	4	5
3	S/he contributes to developing and testing new ways of working	1	2	3	4	5
4	During a period of change s/he has a clear documented plan and actively develops systems to manage the changes aimed for	1	2	3	4	5
5	S/he actively interacts with individuals, families, carers, groups and communities to achieve change and development to improve life opportunities	1	2	3	4	5
6	S/he actively involves service users and carers meaningfully in changes to services and products	1	2	3	4	5
7	S/he builds communication processes that make it safe for people to say what is really on their minds	1	2	3	4	5
8	S/he creates credible processes for collaboration	1	2	3	4	5
9	During the first stage of creating collaborative relationships, s/he takes time to establish common ground among all stakeholders	1	2	3	4	5
10	S/he demonstrates to peers her/his own beliefs that trust is the foundation for successful collaboration for change	1	2	3	4	5

Your score: add up all the numbers scored under behaviour frequency.
Write the number here: _____

Score 50–41: Excellent

Score 40–28: Strong

Score 27–16: Opportunities for development

Score 15–1: Important to develop further

Line manager's comments:

What do you think are your manager's strengths in managing change?

What do you think are your manager's most important areas for being effective in managing change?

What is the relative importance of working on this area to their work at the moment – give any examples.

	Working with people	Seldom	Sometimes	Quite often	Often	Always
1	S/he takes seriously her/his responsibility for coaching and mentoring others	1	2	3	4	5
2	S/he invests adequate time within her/his schedule for people development	1	2	3	4	5
3	S/he is committed to developing people from diverse backgrounds	1	2	3	4	5
4	S/he creates opportunities for people to learn new skills including leadership skills	1	2	3	4	5
5	S/he asks people s/he manages to regularly define their expectations and acts on these	1	2	3	4	5
6	S/he creates a mutually agreed format for people to give feedback on her/his own skills in developing them	1	2	3	4	5
7	S/he allocates work effectively and fairly among members of the team s/he manages	1	2	3	4	5
8	S/he has the strength and resolve to hold others to account for agreed targets and take action where required	1	2	3	4	5
9	S/he assesses her/his staff's performance through the use of observation and feedback	1	2	3	4	5
10	Her/his recruitment and selection activity reflects commitment towards planning the local workforce	1	2	3	4	5

Your score: add up all the numbers scored under behaviour frequency.
Write the number here: _____

Score 50–41: Excellent   Score 40–28: Strong
Score 27–16: Opportunities for   Score 15–1: Important to develop
development   further

Line manager's comments:
What do you think are your manager's strengths in working with individuals and teams?
What do you think are her/his most important areas for improvement in developing people?
What is the relative importance of working on this area to their work at the moment – give any examples.

	Using resources	Seldom	Sometimes	Quite often	Often	Always
1	S/he is confident in preparing a financial budget and planning for the acquisition of resources	1	2	3	4	5
2	S/he effectively monitors the budget and takes action where there are unforeseen consequences	1	2	3	4	5
3	S/he knows how to draw on financial expertise both internally and externally where necessary	1	2	3	4	5
4	S/he knows how to work with others to achieve capacity and sustainability around the use of shared resources	1	2	3	4	5
5	S/he uses technological expertise to access and manage information systems concerning resources	1	2	3	4	5
6	S/he contributes to the well-being and productivity of staff in everyday practice	1	2	3	4	5
7	S/he is confident in her/his knowledge and use of health and safety legislation and procedures	1	2	3	4	5
8	S/he actively designs and contributes to procedures to decrease risk and improve the organization's reputation	1	2	3	4	5
9	S/he exercises his/her role in assisting in the commissioning, procurement and monitoring of services and provision	1	2	3	4	5
10	S/he regularly evaluates information within the service in order to review the use of resources	1	2	3	4	5

Your score: add up all the numbers scored under behaviour frequency.
Write the number here: _____

Score 50–41: Excellent

Score 40–28: Strong

Score 27–16: Opportunities for development

Score 15–1: Important to develop further

Line manager's comments:

What do you think are your manager's strengths in managing resources?

What do you think are her/his most important areas for improvement in managing budgets?

What is the relative importance of working on this area to the work at the moment – give any examples.

	Achieving results	Seldom	Sometimes	Quite often	Often	Always
1	S/he is confident in planning objectives for the service and making plans to meet them	1	2	3	4	5
2	The stakeholders s/he works with are satisfied with the way s/he works to meet shared objectives	1	2	3	4	5
3	S/he is confident in how to develop a business plan for her/his service	1	2	3	4	5
4	S/he actively seeks information in order to understand the 'market' and to ensure this is shared to enhance decision making	1	2	3	4	5
5	S/he communicates and agrees with service users on how to work together to improve the service	1	2	3	4	5
6	S/he regularly liaises and works in partnership with other professionals to optimize outcomes for service users	1	2	3	4	5
7	The information systems developed in her/his team allow her/him to identify service users' feedback on the service they receive	1	2	3	4	5
8	S/he has developed and regularly uses clear measures that tell me about the quality of the service	1	2	3	4	5
9	S/he is able to physically demonstrate how the service contributes to the overall performance of the organization	1	2	3	4	5
10	S/he is able to demonstrate how s/he works in partnerships with others to develop, take forward and evaluation direction, policies and strategies in our service area	1	2	3	4	5

Your score: add up all the numbers scored under behaviour frequency.
Write the number here: _____

Score 50–41: Excellent

Score 40–28: Strong

Score 27–16: Opportunities for development

Score 15–1: Important to develop further

Line manager's comments:
What do you think are your manager's strengths in managing quality and performance in your service area?

What do you think are her/his most important areas in enhancing the quality and performance of your service?

What is the relative importance of working on this area to the work at the moment – give any examples.

	Embedded values and principles	Seldom	Sometimes	Quite often	Often	Always
1	S/he is seen as someone who inspires staff to get the most out of their skills and knowledge	1	2	3	4	5
2	S/he always challenges discrimination and harassment in the work place	1	2	3	4	5
3	S/he values the people s/he manages and actively encourages their potential	1	2	3	4	5
4	S/he is in touch with service users' issues and has a means of establishing and understanding their needs	1	2	3	4	5
5	S/he provides an environment in which staff can develop reflective skills and practice	1	2	3	4	5
6	S/he takes responsibility for her/his own continuing professional development	1	2	3	4	5
7	S/he takes responsibility for the professional development of others s/he manages	1	2	3	4	5
8	S/he develops purposeful joint working relationships and partnerships with others	1	2	3	4	5
9	S/he actively develops partnership with service users	1	2	3	4	5
10	S/he has developed plans to address specific issues of discrimination within our service area	1	2	3	4	5

Your score: add up all the numbers scored under behaviour frequency.
Write the number here: _____

Score 50–41: Excellent
Score 27–16: Opportunities for development

Score 40–28: Strong
Score 15–1: Important to develop further

Line manager's comments:

What do you think are your manager's strengths in promoting values in your service?

What do you think are the most important areas for promoting diversity and inclusion in your service?

What is the relative importance of working on this area to their work at the moment – give any examples.

✓

Summary comments – to be completed by the line manager

Following the above exercise what areas did you prioritize as needing most attention?

[   ]

What learning opportunities might be available for your manager over the next year to enable her/him to give these areas attention?

[   ]

Who can help and support the manager in developing a plan to address these?

[   ]

Date completed: _____

Name: _____ Role: _____

Signature: _____

Multi-source feedback tool 3: Proforma for gaining feedback from your peers

Dear colleague,

Thank you for agreeing to participate in contributing to feedback on my management skills. This questionnaire has been designed to help me obtain planned feedback from you on my current skills and complements similar questionnaires that have been completed by others, for example, myself, the staff that I manage, my own line manager and service users [delete as appropriate]. This will enable me to get more rounded feedback from different perspectives. I would be very grateful if you could take the time to complete this questionnaire in the most honest and constructive way possible. The time suggested to complete it is around 30 minutes.

The information given in this questionnaire will be kept anonymous and confidential. The information you give will not be discussed with you after you have completed the questionnaire and will be used for my own purposes only and shared with my learning mentor.

Please circle the frequency level which you think is relevant to me in each area of management behaviour and skill, which have been adapted from the national Leadership and Management Standards. If you are unable to comment on specific questions, please leave blank.

You are not required to put your name on this form.

	Managing self and personal skills	Seldom	Sometimes	Quite often	Often	Always
1	S/he reviews his/her work performance against agreed objectives	1	2	3	4	5
2	S/he makes sure his/her practice fits into the overall vision and objectives of the organization s/he works in	1	2	3	4	5
4	S/he recognizes the effect of her/his emotions on relationships at work	1	2	3	4	5
5	S/he is deeply motivated to make improvements to the services s/he is responsible for	1	2	3	4	5
10	S/he recognizes her/his personal impact on group dynamics	1	2	3	4	5

Thank you, and are there any comments that you would like to add?

	Facilitating change	Seldom	Sometimes	Quite often	Often	Always
1	S/he creates a climate where people can think creatively about practice, systems and processes	1	2	3	4	5
2	S/he encourages people to be innovative and actively supports their ideas	1	2	3	4	5
3	S/he contributes to developing and testing new ways of working	1	2	3	4	5
4	During a period of change s/he has a clear documented plan and actively develops systems to manage the changes aimed for	1	2	3	4	5
5	S/he actively interacts with individuals, families, carers, groups and communities to achieve change and development to improve life opportunities	1	2	3	4	5
6	S/he actively involves service users and carers meaningfully in changes to services and products	1	2	3	4	5
7	S/he builds communication processes that make it safe for people to say what is really on their minds	1	2	3	4	5
8	S/he creates credible processes for collaboration	1	2	3	4	5
9	During the first stage of creating collaborative relationships, s/he takes time to establish common ground among all stakeholders	1	2	3	4	5
10	S/he demonstrates to peers her/his own beliefs that trust is the foundation for successful collaboration for change	1	2	3	4	5

Are there any comments that you would like to add?

	Working with people	Seldom	Sometimes	Quite often	Often	Always
1	S/he asks people s/he manages to regularly define their expectations and acts on these	1	2	3	4	5
2	S/he creates a mutually agreed format for people to give feedback on her/his own skills in developing them	1	2	3	4	5
3	S/he has the strength and resolve to hold others to account for agreed targets and take action where required	1	2	3	4	5

Are there any comments you would like to add?

	Using resources	Seldom	Sometimes	Quite often	Often	Always
1	S/he knows how to work with others to achieve capacity and sustainability around the use of shared resources	1	2	3	4	5
2	S/he actively designs and contributes to procedures to decrease risk and improve the organization's reputation	1	2	3	4	5
3	S/he exercises his/her role in assisting in the commissioning, procurement and monitoring of services and provision	1	2	3	4	5
4	S/he regularly evaluates information within the service in order to review the use of resources	1	2	3	4	5

Are there any comments that you would like to add?

	Achieving results	Seldom	Sometimes	Quite often	Often	Always
1	S/he is confident in planning objectives for the service and making plans to meet them	1	2	3	4	5
2	The stakeholders s/he works with are satisfied with the way s/he works to meet our shared objectives	1	2	3	4	5
3	S/he actively seeks information in order to understand the 'market' and ensure this is shared to enhance decision making	1	2	3	4	5
4	S/he communicates and agrees with service users on how to work together to improve the service	1	2	3	4	5
5	S/he regularly liaises and works in partnership with other professionals to optimize outcomes for service users	1	2	3	4	5
6	S/he is able to demonstrate how s/he works in partnerships with others to develop, take forward and evaluate direction, policies and strategies in our service area	1	2	3	4	5

Are there any comments that you would like to add?

	Embedded values and principles	Seldom	Sometimes	Quite often	Often	Always
1	S/he is seen as someone who inspires staff to get the most out of their skills and knowledge	1	2	3	4	5
2	S/he always challenges discrimination and harassment in the work place	1	2	3	4	5
3	S/he values the people s/he manages and actively encourages their potential	1	2	3	4	5
4	S/he is in touch with service users' issues and has a means of establishing and understanding their needs	1	2	3	4	5
5	S/he develops purposeful joint working relationships and partnerships with others	1	2	3	4	5
6	S/he actively develops partnership with service users	1	2	3	4	5
7	S/he has developed plans to address specific issues of discrimination within our service area	1	2	3	4	5

Are there any comments that you would like to add?

For the recipient manager's use only – summary sheet

Following the above exercise, which areas did you do well in and which areas did you prioritize as needing more or most attention?

Multi-source feedback tool 4: Proforma for gaining feedback from the multi-disciplinary team

Dear colleague,

Thank you for agreeing to participate in contributing to feedback on my management skills. This questionnaire has been designed to help me obtain planned feedback from you on my current skills and complements similar questionnaires that have been completed by others, for example, myself, the staff that I manage, my peers and service users [delete as appropriate]. This will enable me to get more rounded feedback from different perspectives. I would be very grateful if you could take the time to complete this questionnaire in the most honest and constructive way possible. The time suggested to complete it is around 30 minutes.

Please circle the frequency level which you think is relevant to me in each area of management behaviour and skill which have been adapted from the national Leadership and Management Standards. If you are unable to comment on specific questions, please leave blank.

You are not required to put your name on this form.

	Managing self and personal skills	Seldom	Sometimes	Quite often	Often	Always
1	S/he reviews his/her work performance against agreed objectives	1	2	3	4	5
2	S/he makes sure his/her practice fits into the overall vision and objectives of the organization s/he works in	1	2	3	4	5
4	S/he recognizes the effect of her/his emotions on relationships at work	1	2	3	4	5
5	S/he is deeply motivated to make improvements to the services s/he is responsible for	1	2	3	4	5
10	S/he recognizes her/his personal impact on group dynamics	1	2	3	4	5

Thank you, are there any comments that you would like to add?

✓

	Facilitating change	Seldom	Sometimes	Quite often	Often	Always
1	S/he creates a climate where people can think creatively about practice, systems and processes	1	2	3	4	5
2	S/he encourages people to be innovative and actively supports their ideas	1	2	3	4	5
3	S/he contributes to developing and testing new ways of working	1	2	3	4	5
4	During a period of change s/he has a clear documented plan and actively develops systems to manage the changes aimed for	1	2	3	4	5
5	S/he actively interacts with individuals, families, carers, groups and communities to achieve change and development to improve life opportunities	1	2	3	4	5
6	S/he actively involves service users and carers meaningfully in changes to services and products	1	2	3	4	5
7	S/he builds communication processes that make it safe for people to say what is really on their minds	1	2	3	4	5
8	S/he creates credible processes for collaboration	1	2	3	4	5
9	During the first stage of creating collaborative relationships, s/he takes time to establish common ground among all stakeholders	1	2	3	4	5
10	S/he demonstrates to peers her/his own beliefs that trust is the foundation for successful collaboration for change	1	2	3	4	5

Are there any comments that you would like to add?

	Working with people	Seldom	Sometimes	Quite often	Often	Always
1	S/he asks people s/he manages to regularly define their expectations and acts on these	1	2	3	4	5
2	S/he creates a mutually agreed format for people to give feedback on her/his own skills in developing them	1	2	3	4	5
3	S/he has the strength and resolve to hold others to account for agreed targets and take action where required	1	2	3	4	5

Are there any comments you would like to add?

	Using resources	Seldom	Sometimes	Quite often	Often	Always
1	S/he knows how to work with others to achieve capacity and sustainability around the use of shared resources	1	2	3	4	5
2	S/he actively designs and contributes to procedures to decrease risk and improve the organization's reputation	1	2	3	4	5
3	S/he exercises his/her role in assisting in the commissioning, procurement and monitoring of services and provision	1	2	3	4	5
4	S/he regularly evaluates information within the service in order to review the use of resources	1	2	3	4	5

Are there any comments that you would like to add?

	Achieving results	Seldom	Sometimes	Quite often	Often	Always
1	S/he is confident in planning objectives for the service and making plans to meet them	1	2	3	4	5
2	The stakeholders s/he works with are satisfied with the way s/he works to meet our shared objectives	1	2	3	4	5
3	S/he actively seeks information in order to understand the 'market' and ensure this is shared to enhance decision making	1	2	3	4	5
4	S/he communicates and agrees with service users on how to work together to improve the service	1	2	3	4	5
5	S/he regularly liaises and works in partnership with other professionals to optimize outcomes for service users	1	2	3	4	5
6	S/he is able to demonstrate how s/he works in partnerships with others to develop, take forward and evaluate direction, policies and strategies in our service area	1	2	3	4	5

Are there any comments that you would like to add?

	Embedded values and principles	Seldom	Sometimes	Quite often	Often	Always
1	S/he is seen as someone who inspires staff to get the most out of their skills and knowledge	1	2	3	4	5
2	S/he always challenges discrimination and harassment in the work place	1	2	3	4	5
3	S/he values the people s/he manages and actively encourages their potential	1	2	3	4	5
4	S/he is in touch with service users' issues and has a means of establishing and understanding their needs	1	2	3	4	5
5	S/he develops purposeful joint working relationships and partnerships with others	1	2	3	4	5
6	S/he actively develops partnership with service users	1	2	3	4	5
7	S/he has developed plans to address specific issues of discrimination within our service area	1	2	3	4	5

Are there any comments that you would like to add?

For the recipient manager's use only – self-assessment summary sheet

Following the above exercise, which areas did you do well in and which areas did you prioritize as needing more or most attention?

Multi-source feedback tool 5: Proforma for gaining feedback from service users and carers

Dear [insert name],

Thank you for agreeing to participate in contributing to feedback on my management skills. This questionnaire has been designed to help me obtain planned feedback from you on my current skills and complements similar questionnaires that have been completed by others, for example, myself, the staff that I manage, my peers and my own line manager [delete as appropriate]. This will enable me to get more rounded feedback from different perspectives. I would be very grateful if you could take the time to complete this questionnaire in the most honest and constructive way possible. The time suggested to complete it is around 30 minutes.

If you would like someone to complete this questionnaire with you or would like it in a different format please let me know. Completing this questionnaire will not affect your service in any way, neither are your responses associated with the support you receive. The information given in this questionnaire will be kept anonymous and confidential. The information you give will not be discussed with you after you have completed the questionnaire and will be used for my own purposes only and shared with my learning mentor.

Question 1: When you have contact with staff from my service, what support do you feel they need from the management team in order to do their job in the best way possible?

Question 2: Do you have any views about the way in which managers in our organization relate to service users and what could be done to improve communication and information sharing between us?

Question 3: Do you feel that the resources available to the service you used are used fairly and transparently in the community you live in?

Question 4: What suggestions would you like to make to me as someone who manages your service about how it could be changed in order to improve or how managers and service users might work better together to do this?

Thank you very much for taking the time to complete this – the information will be kept confidential and used for my own self-development purposes only.

Individual Learning and Development Plan

Name of manager: _____

Name of line manager: _____

Name of mentor/coach: _____

1. Outline here the key areas for development highlighted from your multi-source management skills audit.

2. Identify the two most important management skills areas that you have agreed to work on before your next appraisal.

3. How will these be supported by learning opportunities in the workplace? (Who/what/where/when?)

✓

4. Outcome measures – what sources of evidence or indicators will be used to demonstrate any progress?

```
┌─────────────────────────────────────────────────────┐
│                                                       │
│                                                       │
│                                                       │
│                                                       │
│                                                       │
└─────────────────────────────────────────────────────┘
```

5. Agreed methods for giving and receiving feedback (to be completed by your line manager).

```
┌─────────────────────────────────────────────────────┐
│                                                       │
│                                                       │
│                                                       │
│                                                       │
│                                                       │
└─────────────────────────────────────────────────────┘
```

6. Any significant dates for review:

```
┌─────────────────────────────────────────────────────┐
│                                                       │
│                                                       │
│                                                       │
│                                                       │
│                                                       │
└─────────────────────────────────────────────────────┘
```

Signed: _____

Signed: _____

Signed: _____

References

Aberbach, J.D. and Christensen, T. (2005) 'Citizens and consumers: An NPM dilemma.' *Public Management Review 7*, 2, 225–245.

ACAS (2009) *Managing Conflict at Work.* Available online from www.acas.org.uk/publications.

Alimo-Metcalfe, B. and Alban-Metcalfe, J. (2006) 'More (good) leaders for the public sector.' *International Journal of Public Sector Management 19*, 4, 293–315.

Armenakis, A. and Harris, S. (2009) 'Reflections: Our journey in organizational change research and practice.' *Journal of Change Management 9*, 2, 127–142.

Armstrong, D. (2004) 'Emotions in Organizations: Disturbance or Intelligence.' In C. Huffington, D. Armstrong, W. Halton, L. Hoyle and J. Pooley (eds) *Working below the Surface: The Emotional Life of Contemporary Organizations.* London: Karnac.

Arnstein, S.R. (1969) 'A ladder of citizen participation.' *Journal of the American Institute of Planners 35*, 4, 216–224. Available at http://lithgow-schmidt.dk/sherry-arnstein/ladder-of-citizen-participation.pdf, accessed October 2011.

Aronson, J. and Smith, K. (2009) 'Managing restructured social services: Expanding the social?' *British Journal of Social Work 40*, 2, 530–547.

Attwood, M., Pedler, M., Pritchard, S. and Wilkinson, D. (2003) *Leading Change: A Guide to Whole Systems Working.* Bristol: Policy Press.

Baginsky, M., Moriarty, J., Manthorpe, J., Stevens, M., MacInnes, T. and Nagendran, T. (2010) *Social Workers' Workload Survey. Messages from the Frontline. Findings from the 2009 Survey and Interviews with Senior Managers.* London: Department for Children, Schools and Families/Department of Health.

Banks, P. (2002) *Partnerships under Pressure: A Commentary on Progress in Partnership-working between the NHS and Local Government.* London: King's Fund.

Banks, S. (2006) *Ethics and Values in Social Work.* Basingstoke: Palgrave Macmillan.

Barnes, C., Mercer, G. and Din, I. (2003) *Research Review on User Involvement in Promoting Change and Enhancing the Quality of Social 'Care' Services for Disabled People.* Final report for SCIE. Leeds: Centre for Disability Studies, University of Leeds.

Barnes, M. (2002) 'Taking over the asylum.' Paper for the Critical Psychiatry Network Conference, Birmingham, 26 April. Available at www.critpsynet.freeuk.com/Barnes.htm, accessed October 2011.

Baulcombe, S., Edwards, S., Hostick, T., New, A. and Pugh, K. (2001) *Asking The Experts' – A Guide To Involving People in Shaping Health and Social Care Services.* Brigg, North Lincolnshire: CCNAP.

Bell, K. and Smerdon, M. (2011) *Deep Value: A Literature Review of the Role of Effective Relationships in Public Services.* London: Community Links. Available at www.community-links.org/our-national-work/publications/deep-value, accessed October 2011.

Bell M. (2002) Promoting children's rights through the use of relationship. *Child and Family Social Work 7*, 1, 1–11.

Benner, P. (1984) *From Novice to Expert: Excellence and Power in Clinical Nursing Practice.* Menlo Park, CA: Addison-Wesley,

Beresford, P. and Croft, S (2001) 'Service users' knowledges and the social construction of social work.' *Journal of Social Work 1*, 3, 295–316.

Beresford, P., Bewley, C., Branfield, F., Croft, S. *et al.* (2011) *Supporting People: Towards a Person-centred Approach.* Bristol: Policy Press.

Binney, G., Wilke, G. and Williams, G. (2005) *Living Leadership.* London: Prentice Hall and Financial Times.

Birkinshaw, J. and Gibson, C. (2005) *The Ambidextrous Organisation.* London: Economic & Social Research Council. Available at www.aimresearch.org/uploads/File/pdf/Executive%20Briefing/Ambidexterous%20org%20Exec%20Briefing-%20FINAL%20Sept%2005.pdf, accessed October 2011.

Boehm, A. and Yoels, N. (2008) 'Effectiveness of welfare organisations: The contribution of leadership styles, staff cohesion, and worker empowerment.' *British Journal of Social Work 39*, 7, 1360–1380.

Bourn, D. and Hafford-Letchfield, T. (2011) 'Professional supervision in conditions of uncertainty.' *International Journal of Knowledge, Culture and Change Management 10*, 9, 41–56.

Bowen, D.E. and Schneider, B. (1988) 'Organizing principles for service organizations.' *Research in Organizational Behaviour 10*, 55–69.

Branfield, F. and Beresford, P. (2006) *Making User Involvement Work: Supporting Service User Networking and Knowledge*. York: Joseph Rowntree Foundation.

Brockbank, A. and McGill, I. (2006) *Facilitating Reflective Learning through Mentoring and Coaching*. London: Kogan Page.

Brodie, E., Cowling. E. and Nissen, N. (2009) *Understanding Participation: A Literature Review*. London: National Council for Voluntary Organisations.

Bryans, P. and Mavin, S. (2003) 'Women learning to become managers: Learning to fit in or to play a different game?' *Management Learning 34*, 1, 111–134.

Burnes, B. and Jackson, P. (2011) 'Success and failure in organizational change: An exploration of the role of values.' *Journal of Change Management 11*, 2, 133–162.

Burton, J. and van der Broek, D. (2008) 'Accountable and countable: Information management systems and the bureaucratization of social work.' *British Journal of Social Work 39*, 7, 1326–1342.

Byford, S. and Sefton, T. (2003) 'Economic evaluation of complex health and social care interventions.' *National Institute Economic Review*, 186.

Cameron, E. and Green, M. (2009) *Making Sense of Change Management; A Complete Guide to the Models, Tools and Techniques of Organizational Change*, 2nd edn. London: Kogan Page.

Campbell, D. and Draper, R. (1985) (eds) *Applications of Systemic Family Therapy, The Milan Approach*. London: Grune and Stratton.

Carpenter, J., McLaughlin, H., Patsios, D., Blewett, J. *et al.* (2010) *Newly Qualified Social Worker Programme: Evaluation of the First Year: 2008–09*. Leeds: Children's Workforce Development Council.

Carr, S. (2004) *Has Service User Participation Made a Difference to Social Care Services?* Position Paper No. 3, Social Care Institute for Excellence. Bristol: Policy Press.

Carr, S. (2007) 'Participation, power, conflict and change: Theorizing dynamics of service user participation in the social care system of England and Wales.' *Critical Social Policy 27*, 2, 266–276.

Cecchin, G. (1987) 'Hypothesizing, circularity, and neutrality revisited: An invitation to curiosity.' *Family Process 26*, 4, 405–413.

Ceeney, N. (2009) 'Information management – Headache or opportunity? – The challenges that the recent focus on information management is presenting to senior leaders in the public sector.' *Public Policy and Administration 24*, 3, 339–347.

Chalfont, G. and Hafford-Letchfield, T. (2010) 'Leadership from the bottom up: Reinventing dementia care in residential and nursing home settings.' *Social Work and Social Sciences Review 14*, 1, 27–46.

Clarke, J. (2004) *Changing Welfare, Changing States, New Directions in Social Policy*. London: Sage.

Clarke, J. and Newman, J. (1997) *The Managerial State: Power, Politics and Ideology in the Remaking of Social Welfare*. London: Sage.

Clutterbuck, D. (1998) *Learning Alliances: Tapping into Talent*. London: IPD.

Clutterbuck, D. and Megginson, D. (1995) *Mentoring in Action: A Practical Guide for Managers*. London: Kogan Page.

Cockburn, C. (1983) *Brothers: Male Dominance and Technological Change*. London: Pluto Press.

Coleman, M. and Earley, P. (2005) *Leadership and Management in Education: Cultures, Change and Context*. Oxford: Oxford University Press.

Conklin, J. (2010) 'Resisting change or preserving value: A case study of resistance to change in a health organization.' *International Journal of Knowledge, Culture and Change Management 10*, 481–493.

Cook, C. (2010) 'The power of peer support.' *Straight Talk 25*, 2, 20–21.

Cornes, M., Gill, L., Armstrong, S. and Bowes, M. (2010a) *Toughness and Emotional Loyalty Training: Impact on Staff Retention Rates in Four Diverse Social Care Provider Organisations in Cumbria: Evaluation Report*. London: Social Care Workforce Research Unit, Kings College London with Care Sector Alliance Cumbria.

Cornes, M., Moriarty, J., Blendi-Mahota, S., Chittleburgh, T., Hussein, S. and Manthorpe, J. (2010b) *Working for the Agency: The Role and Significance of Temporary Employment Agencies in the Adult Social Care Workforce. Final Report to the Department of Health*. London: Social Care Workforce Research Unit, King's College London.

Cornwall, A. (2008) 'Unpacking "participation": Models, meanings and practices.' *Community Development Journal 43*, 3, 269–283.

Covey, S. (2004) *The 7 Habits of Highly Effective People*. London: Simon and Schuster.

Covey, S., Merrill, A.R. and Merrill, R.R. (1994) *First Things First: To Live, to Love, to Learn, to Leave a Legacy*. New York: Simon and Schuster.

Cree, V. and McCaulay, C. (2001) *Transfer of Learning in Professional and Vocational Education*. London: Routledge.

Crisp, C., Anderson, M., Orme, J. and Green Lister, P. (2003) *SCIE Knowledge Review 01: Learning and Teaching Assessment Skills in Social Work Education*. London: Social Care Institute for Excellence.

Darling, L.A.W. (1986) 'What to do about toxic mentors.' *Nurse Educator 11*, 2, 29–30.

Delbridge, R., Gratton, L. and Johnson, G. (2006) *The Exceptional Manager: Making the Difference*. Oxford: Oxford University Press.

Department for Children, Schools and Families (DCSF) (2009) *Building a Safe, Confident Future: The Final Report of the Social Work Task Force*, London: Stationery Office.

Department of Health (2004) *Choosing Health: Making Healthy Choices Easier*. Cm 6374. London: Stationery Office.

Doel, M., Carroll, C., Chambers, E., Cooke, J. *et al.* (2007) *Participation: Finding Out What Difference It Makes*. Project Report. London: Social Care Institute for Excellence. Available at www.scie.org.uk/publications/guides/guide20/index.asp, accessed October 2011.

Doel, M., Shardlow, S. and Sawdon, D. (1996) *Teaching Social Work Practice*. Aldershot: Arena.

Doyle, M., Claydon, T. and Buchanan, D. (2000) 'Mixed results, lousy process: The management experience of organizational change.' *British Journal of Management 11*, S.59–80.

Drucker, P.F. (1993) *Post-capitalist Society*. New York: Harper Business.

Duck, J.D. (1993) 'Managing change: The art of balancing.' *Harvard Business Review* November–December, 109–118.

Dustin, D. (2007) *The McDonaldization of Social Work*. Aldershot: Ashgate.

Egan, G. (1994) *Working the Shadow Side*. San Francisco: Jossey Bass Publishers.

Felstead, A., Gallie, D. and Green, F. (2002). *Work Skills in Britain 1986–2001*. Nottingham: DfES Publications.

Figley, C.R. (1995) *Compassion Fatigue: Coping with Secondary Traumatic Stress Disorder in Those Who Treat the Traumatized*. New York: Brunner/Mazel.

Findlay, P., Findlay, J. and Stewart, R. (2009) 'The consequences of caring: Skills, regulation and reward among early years workers.' *Work Employment and Society 23*, 3, 422–441.

Fletcher, D.R. (2003) 'Employers, recruitment and offenders: Underlining the limits of work-focused welfare?' *Policy and Politics 31*, 4, 497–510.

Ford, J. D., Ford, L.W. and D'Amelio, A. (2008) 'Resistance to change: The rest of the story.' *Academy of Management Review 33*, 362–377.

Forster, M. (2006) *Do It Tomorrow and Other Secrets of Time Management*. London: Hodder and Stoughton.

Forsyth, P. (1991) *How to Negotiate Successfully*. London: Sheldon Press.

Foster-Turner, J. (2006) *Coaching and Mentoring in Health and Social Care*. Abingdon: Radcliffe Publishing.

Fox, S. (1997) 'From Management Education to Management Learning.' In J. Burgoyne and M. Reynolds (eds) *Management Learning: Integrating Perspectives in Theory and Practice*. London: Sage.

Furze, D. and Gale, C. (1996) *Interpreting Management: Exploring Change and Complexity.* London: International Thomson Business Press.

Gallagher, K. (2010) *Skills Development for Management and Business Students.* Buckingham: SRHE and Open University Press.

Gardner, L. and Stough, C. (2002) 'Examining the relationship between leadership and emotional intelligence in senior level managers.' *Leadership and Organization Development Journal 23,* 68–78.

Gaventa, J. (2006) 'Finding the space for change: A power analysis.' *Institute of Development Studies 37,* 6, 23–33.

General Social Care Council (2010) *Specialist Standards and Requirements for Post-qualifying Social Work Education and Training: Leadership and Management.* London: General Social Care Council.

George, J.M. (2000) 'Emotions and leadership: The role of emotional intelligence.' *Human Relations 53,* 1027–1055.

Glendinning, C. (2009) 'The Consumer in Health Care.' In R. Simmons, M. Powell and I. Greener (eds) *The Consumer in Public Services: Choice, Values and Difference.* Bristol: Policy Press.

Glendinning, C., Clarke, S., Hare, P., Maddison, J. and Newbronner, L. (2008) 'Progress and problems in developing outcome focussed social care services for older people in England.' *Health and Social Care in the Community 6,* 1, 54–63.

Goleman, D. (1996) *Emotional Intelligence.* New York: Bantam Books.

Goleman, D. (1998) *Working with Emotional Intelligence.* New York: Bantam Books.

Gould, N. (2000) 'Becoming a learning organisation: A social work example.' *Social Work Education 19,* 6, 585–596.

Graetz, F. and Smith, C.T. (2010) 'Managing organizational change: A philosophies of change approach.' *Journal of Change Management 10,* 2, 135–154.

Hafford-Letchfield, T. (2009) *Management and Organisations in Social* Work, 2nd edn. Exeter: Learning Matters.

Hafford-Letchfield, T. (2010) *Social Care Management: Strategy and Business Planning.* London: Jessica Kingsley Publishers.

Hafford-Letchfield, T. (2011) 'Women and Sexuality in Care Organisations: Negotiating Boundaries within a Gendered Cultural Script.' In P. Dunk-West and T. Hafford-Letchfield (eds) *Sexuality and Sexual Identities in Social Work, Reflections from Women in the Field.* Aldershot: Ashgate Press.

Hafford-Letchfield, T. (in press) 'Funny things happen at the Grange: Introducing comedy activities in day services to older people with dementia.' *Dementia: International Journal of Social Research and Practice.*

Hafford-Letchfield, T. and Bourn, D. (2011) '"How am I doing?" Advancing management skills through the use of a multi-source feedback tool to enhance work-based learning on a post-qualifying post-graduate leadership and management programme.' *Social Work Education 30,* 5, 495–511.

Hafford-Letchfield, T. and Chick, N. F (2006) 'Talking across purposes: The benefits of an inter-agency mentoring scheme for managers working in health and social care settings in the UK.' *Work Based Learning in Primary Care 4,* 13–24.

Hafford-Letchfield, T., Chick, N.F., Leonard, K. and Begum, N. (2008) *Leadership and Management in Social Care.* London: Sage.

Hafford-Letchfield, T., Couchman, W., Webster, M. and Avery, P. (2010) 'A drama project about older people's intimacy and sexuality.' *Educational Gerontology 36,* 7, 1–18.

Handy, C. (1990) *Inside Organisations.* London: Penguin.

Handy, C. (1999) *Understanding Organizations,* (4th edition). New York, Oxford: Oxford University Press.

Harris, J. (1998) 'Scientific management, bureau-professionalism, new managerialism: The labour process of state social work.' *British Journal of Social Work 28,* 839–862.

Harris, J., Manthorpe, J. and Hussein, S. (2008) *What Works in 'Grow Your Own' Initiatives for Social Work: Research Report.* London: General Social Care Council.

Hart, R.A. (1997) *Children's Participation: The Theory and Practice of Involving Young Citizens in Community Development and Environmental Care.* London: Earthscan.

Hay, J. (1995) *Transformational Mentoring*. Maidenhead: McGraw-Hill.

Hay, J. (2009) *Working It Out at Work*. Watford: Sherwood Publishing.

Healy, K. (2002) 'Managing human services in a market environment; what role for social workers?' *British Journal of Social Work 32*, 5, 527–540.

Hearn, J. and Parkin, W. (2001) *Gender, Sexuality and Violence in Organizations*. London: Sage.

Heller, J. (1994) *Catch 22*. London: Random House. (Original work published in 1955.)

HM Government (2007) *Putting People First: A Shared Vision and Commitment to the Transformation of Adult Social Care*. London: HMG.

Higgs, M. and Rowland, D. (2010) 'Emperors with clothes on: The role of self-awareness in developing effective change leadership.' *Journal of Change Management 10*, 4, 369–385.

Higgs, M. and Rowland, D. (2011) 'What does it take to implement change successfully? A study of the behaviors of successful change leaders.' *Journal of Applied Behavioral Science 20*, 10, 1–27.

Higgs, M.J. and Rowland, D. (2005). 'All changes great and small: Exploring approaches to change and its leadership.' *Journal of Change Management 5*, 2, 121–151.

Holmes, L., McDermid, S., Jones, A. and Ward, H. (2009) *How Social Workers Spend Their Time: An Analysis of the Key Issues that Impact on practice Pre- and Post Implementation of the Integrated Children's System*. Loughborough: Department for Children, Schools and Families.

Holt, J. and Lawler, J. (2005) 'Children in Need Teams: Service delivery and organizational climate.' *Social Work and Social Sciences Review 12*, 2, 29–47.

Honey P. (1991) 'The learning organisation simplified' *Training and Development, 9*, 7, 30–33.

Honey, P. (2001) *Improve your people skills*, 2nd edn. London: Chartered Institute of Personnel and Development.

Horwath, J. and Morrison, T. (2000) 'Identifying and implementing pathways for organizational change – using the *Framework for the Assessment of Children in Need and their Families* as a case example.' *Child and Family Social Work 5*, 3, 245–254.

House of Commons Public Administration Select Committee (2008) *Public Administration Select Committee: User Involvement in Public Services*. London: Stationery Office. Available at www.parliament.the-stationery-office.co.uk/pa/cm20 0708/cmselect/cmpubadm/410/410.pdf, accessed October 2011.

Howe, D. (2008) *The Emotionally Intelligent Social Worker*. Basingstoke: Palgrave Macmillan.

Hoyle, L. (2004) 'Clash of the Titans – conflict resolution using a contextualised mediation process.' In C. Huffington, D. Armstrong, W. Halton, L. Hoyle and J. Pooley (eds) *Working below the Surface: The Emotional Life of Contemporary Organizations*. London: Karnac.

Huffington, C., Armstrong, D., Halton, W., Hoyle, L. and Pooley, J. (2004) *Working below the Surface: The Emotional Life of Contemporary Organizations*. London: Karnac.

Hussein, S., Stevens, M. and Manthorpe, J., (2010) *International Social Care Workers in England: Profile, Motivations, Experiences and Future Expectations: Final Report*. London: Social Care Workforce Research Unit, King's College London.

Improvement and Development Agency (2008) *Lessons from Outsourcing Adult Social Care: The Workforce Issues*. London: Social Care Workforce Research Unit.

Involve (2005) *People and Participation – How to Put Citizens at the Heart of Decision-making*. London: Involve.

Janis, I. (1972) *Victims of Groupthink; A Psychological Study of Foreign-Policy Decisions and Fiascoes*. Boston: Houghton, Mifflin.

Johnson, K. and Williams, I. (2007) *Managing Uncertainty and Change in Social Work and Social Care*. Lyme Regis: Russell House Publishing.

Jones, C. (2001) 'Voices from the front line: state social workers and New Labour.' *British Journal of Social Work, 31*, 547–562.

Jones, R. (2008) 'Expert view: Safety is a stable frontline.' *Guardian*, 26 Nov. Available at www.guardian.co.uk/society/2008/nov/26/baby-p-child-protection-ray-jones, accessed October 2011.

Kadushin, A. and Harkness, D. (2002) *Supervision in Social Work*, 4th edn. New York: Columbia University.

Kane, J. (1999) 'Job sharing: a retention strategy for nurses.' *Canadian Journal of Nursing Leadership 12*, 4, 16–22.

Kotter, J.P. (1996) *Leading Change*. Boston: Harvard Business School Press.

Kotter, J.P. and Cohen, D.S. (2002) *The Heart of Change: Real-life Stories of How People Change Their Organizations*. Boston: Harvard Business School Press.

Kouzes, J.M. and Mico, P.R. (1979) 'Domain Theory: An introduction to organizational behaviour in human service organizations.' *Journal of Applied Behavioural Science 15*, 4, 449–469.

Kraybill, K. (2003) *Creating and Maintaining a Healthy Work Environment: A Resource Guide for Staff Retreats, National Health Care for the Homeless Council and Health Care for the Homeless Clinicians' Network*. Available at www.nhchc.org/Clinicians/ResourceGuideforStaffRetreats.pdf, accessed October 2011.

Laming, H.E. (2009) *The Protection of Children in England: A Progress Report*. London: Stationery Office.

Lave, J. and Wenger, E. (1991) *Situated Learning: Legitimate Peripheral Participation*. Cambridge: Cambridge University Press.

Lawler, J. and Bilson, A. (2010) *Social Work Management and Leadership: Managing Complexity with Creativity*. Oxford and New York: Routledge.

Lee, T., Fuller, A., Ashton, D., Butler, P. *et al.* (2004) *Workplace Learning: Main Themes and Perspectives*, Learning as Work Research Paper No 2. Leicester: Centre for Labour Market Studies, University of Leicester.

Leslie, K. and Canwell, A. (2010) 'Leadership at all levels: Leading public sector organisations in an age of austerity.' *European Management Journal 28*, 4, 297–305.

Lewin, K. (1951) *Field Theory in Social Science*. New York: Harper and Row.

Lymbery, M. (2001) 'Social work at the crossroads.' *British Journal of Social Work 31*, 3, 369–384.

Lymbery, M. (2003) 'Negotiating the contradictions between competence and creativity in social work education.' *Journal of Social Work 3*, 1, 99–117.

MacDonald, L.A.C. (2005) *Wellness at Work: Protecting and Promoting Employee Health and Well-Being*. London: Chartered Institute of Personnel.

Maddock, S. (1999) *Challenging Women: Gender, Culture and Organisation*. London: Sage.

Mannion, R., Davies, H., Harrison, S., Konteh, F. *et al.* (2010) *Changing Management Cultures and Organizational Performance in the NHS (OC2)*. Available at www.sdo.nihr.ac.uk/files/project/94-final-report.pdf, accessed October 2011.

Mannion, R., Davies, H., Konteh, F., Jung, T. *et al.* (2008) *Measuring and Assessing Organizational Culture in the NHS*. Available at www.sdo.nihr.ac.uk/files/adhoc/91–research-summary.pdf, accessed October 2011.

Manthorpe, J., Martineau S.A., Moriarty, J., Hussein, S. and Stevens, M. (2010) 'Support workers in social care in England: A scoping study.' *Health and Social Care in the Community 18*, 3, 316–324.

Marris, P. (1986) *Loss and Change*. London: Kogan Paul.

Maslow, A.H. (1943) 'A Theory of Human Motivation', *Psychological Review 50*, 4, 370–96.

Mason, B. (1993) 'Towards positions of safe uncertainty.' *Human Systems 4*, 3, 189–200.

McLaughlin, H. (2009) 'What's in a name: 'client', 'patient', 'customer', 'consumer', 'expert by experience', 'service user'–What's next?' *British Journal of Social Work 39*, 6, 1101–1017.

Megginson, D. and Clutterbuck, D. (2005) *Techniques for Coaching and Mentoring*. Oxford: Elsevier Butterworth Heinemann.

Megginson, D. and Clutterbuck, D. (2009) *Further Techniques for Coaching and Mentoring*. Oxford: Elsevier Butterworth Heinemann.

Megginson, D., Clutterbuck, D., Garvey, B., Stokes, P. and Garrett-Harris, R. (2006) *Mentoring in Action*, 2nd edn. London: Kogan Page.

Miller, D. (2002) 'Successful change leaders: What makes them? What do they do that is different?' *Journal of Change Management 2*, 4, 359–368.

Morgan, G. (1993) *Imaginization*. Beverly Hills, CA: Sage.

Moriarty, J., Rapaport, P., Beresford, P., Branfield, F. *et al.* (2007) *Practice Guide. The Participation of Adult Service Users, Including Older People, in Developing Social Care.* London: Social Care Institute for Excellence.

Morrison, T. (2007) 'Emotional intelligence, emotion and social work: Context, characteristics, complications and contribution.' *British Journal of Social Work 37,* 2, 245–263.

Morton-Cooper, A. and Palmer, A. (2000) *Mentoring, Preceptorship and Clinical Supervision: A Guide to Professional Support Roles in Clinical Practice.* Oxford: Blackwell Science.

Moss, B. (2007) *Values.* Lyme Regis: Russell House Publishing.

Munro, E. (2010) *The Munro Review of Child Protection Part One: A Systems Analysis.* Department of Education, London: Stationery Office.

Munro, E. (2011) *The Munro Review of Child Protection: Final Report, A Child-centred System Report.* Department of Education, London: Stationery Office.

Mustafa, N. (2008) 'How the United Kingdom's Criminal Records Bureau can reduce the prevalence of elder abuse by improving recruitment decision-making.' *Journal of Adult Protection 10,* 4, 37–45.

Nakhnikian, E. and Kahn, K. (2004) *Direct care Workers Speaking Out on their Own Behalf.* Washington, DC: Institute for the Future of Aging Services.

Needham, C. and Carr, S. (2009) Co-production: an emerging evidence base for adult social care transformation, *Research Briefing 31,* London: Social Care Institute for Excellence.

Newbronner, L., Chamberlain, R., Bosanquet, K., Bartlett, C., Sass, B. and Glendinning, C. (2011) *Keeping Personal Budgets Personal: Learning from the Experiences of Older People, People with Mental Health Problems and their Carers.* Adults' Services Report, 40. London: Social Care Institute for Excellence. Available at http://php.york.ac.uk/inst/spru/pubs/1920, accessed October 2011.

Noble, J., Harris, J. and Manthorpe, J. (2009) *Grow Your Own Social Workers: A Toolkit.* London: General Social Care Council.

Nonaka, I. (1991) 'The Knowledge Creating Company', *Harvard Business Review 69,* 6, 96–104.

Oliver, M. (1983) *Social Work with Disabled People.* Basingstoke: Macmillan.

Owen, H. (2008) *Open Space Technology: A User's Guide.* 3rd edn. San Francisco: Berrett-Koehler

Parsloe, E. and Wray, M. (2000) *Coaching and Mentoring: Practical Methods to Improve Learning.* London: Kogan Page.

Pearson, C., Watson, N., Stalker, K., Lerpiniere, J., Paterson, K. and Ferrie, J. (2011) 'Don't get involved: An examination of how public sector organisations in England are involving disabled people in the Disability Equality Duty.' *Disability and Society 6,* 3, 255–268.

Pedler, M., Burgoyne, J. and Boydell, T. (1991) *The Learning Company: A Strategy for Sustainable Development.* London: McGraw-Hill.

Pemberton, S. and Mason, J. (2008) 'Co-production and Sure Start Children's Centres: Reflecting upon users perspectives and implications for service planning, delivery and evaluation', *Social Policy and Society 8,* 1, 13–24.

Performance and Innovation Unit (2001) *Strengthening Leadership in the Public Sector: A Research Study by the PIU.* London: Performance Innovation Unit.

Perlow, L.A. (1999) 'The time famine: towards a sociology of work time.' *Administrative Science Quarterly 44,* 1, 57–81.

Perry, R. W. (2004) 'The Impact of Criminal Conviction Disclosure on the Self-reported Offending Profile of Social Work Students', *British Journal of Social Work 34,* 7, 997–1008.

Pettinger, R. (2001) *Mastering Management Skills.* Basingstoke: Palgrave McMillan.

Pfeffer, J. and Sutton, R.I. (2006) *Hard Facts, Dangerous Half-Truths and Total Nonsense: Profiting from Evidence-Based Management.* Boston: Harvard Business School Press.

Phillipson, J. (1998) *Piecing Together the Jigsaws.* London: CCETSW.

Pine, B. and Healy, L. (2007) 'New Leadership for the Human Services'. In, J. Aldgate, L. Healy, B. Malcolm, B. Pine, W. Rose and J. Seden (eds) *Enhancing Social Work Management,* London: Jessica Kingsley Publishers.

Preston-Shoot, M. (2009) 'Observations on the Development of Law and Policy for Integrated Practice.' In J. McKimm and J. Phillips (2003) *Leadership and Management of Integrated Services.* Exeter: Learning Matters.

Pritchard, J. (2000) 'Training for conflict.' *Community Care,* 26 Jan.

Prosser, S. (2010) *Effective People: Leadership and Organisation Development in Healthcare.* Auckland, New Zealand: Pindar.

Rees, W.D. and Porter, C. (1996) *Skills of Management,* 5th edn. London: Thomson.

Reynolds, J., Henderson J., Seden J., Charlesworth J. and Bullman, A. (eds). *The Managing Care Reader.* London: Routledge.

Robson, C. (2002) *Real World Research* 2nd edn. London: Blackwells Publishing.

Rogers, A. and Reynolds, J. (2003) 'Managing Change'. In Seden, J. and Reynolds, J. (eds) (2003) *Managing Care in Practice.* London: Routledge.

Roulstone, A., Hudson, V., Kearney, J. and Martin, A. (2006) *Working Together: Carer Participation in England, Wales and Northern Ireland.* London: Social Care Institute for Excellence. Available at www.scie.org.uk/publications/positionpapers/pp05.pdf, accessed October 2011.

Routledge, M. and Sanderson, H. (2000) *Work in Progress: Implementing Person Centred Planning in Oldham.* Clitheroe: North West Training and Development. Available at www.nwtdt.com/Archive/pcp/docs/PCPsept17.PDF, accessed October 2011.

Rumsey, H. (1995) *Mentors in Post Qualifying Education; an Inter-professional Perspective.* London: CCETSW.

Sainsbury Centre for Mental Health (2010) *An Evaluation of Mental Health Service User Involvement in the Recommissioning of Day and Vocational Services.* Available at www.centreformentalhealth.org.uk/publications/references.aspx, accessed October 2011.

Schön, D. (1987) *The Reflective Practitioner.* New York: Basic Books.

Scott, J., Gill, A. and Crowhurst, K. (2008) *Effective Management in Long-term Care Organisations.* Exeter: Reflect Press.

Senge, P. (1990) *The Fifth Discipline: The Art and Practice of the Learning Organization.* New York: Doubleday.

Shapiro, J.J. and Hughes, S.K. (1996) 'Information literacy as a liberal art.' *Educom Review 31,* 2, 31–35.

Simmons, R. (2009) 'Understanding the "Differentiated Consumer" in Public Services.' In R. Simmons, M. Powell and I. Greener (2009) (eds) *The Consumer in Public Services: Choice, Values and Difference.* Bristol: Policy Press.

Simmons, R., Powell, M. and Greener, I. (2009) (eds) *The Consumer in Public Services: Choice, Values and Difference.* Bristol: Policy Press.

Simpson, E.L., House, A.O. and Barkham, M. (2002) *A Guide to Involving Users, Ex-users and Carers in Mental Health Service Planning, Delivery or Research: A Health Technology Approach.* Leeds: Academic Unit of Psychiatry and Behavioural Sciences, University of Leeds.

Skills for Care (2006) *Strategic Uses of National Occupational Standards.* Leeds: Skills for Care.

Skills for Care (2008a) *Adult Social Care Manager Induction Standards.* Leeds: Skills for Care.

Skills for Care (2008b) *Mapping of Leadership and Management Standards for Health and Social Care, Leadership and Management Product 3,* 2nd edn. London: Skills for Care.

Skills for Care (2009) *Developing Integrated Local Area Workforce Strategies: Opportunities and Challenges.* Leeds: Skills for Care.

Skills for Care (2010a) *Men into Care – A Research-based Contribution to a Recruitment and Retention Issue.* Leeds: Skills for Care.

Skills for Care (2010b) *Finders, Keepers: The Adult Social Care Sector Recruitment and Retention Toolkit.* Leeds: Skills for Care.

Skinner, D., Saunders, M.N.K. and Beresford, R. (2004) 'Towards a shared understanding of skill shortages: Differing perceptions of training and developing needs.' *Education and Training 46,* 4, 182–193.

Smale, G. (1996) *Mapping Change and Innovation.* London: HMSO.

Smale, G. (1998) *Managing Change through Innovation.* London: Stationery Office.

Smale, G., Tuson, G. and Statham, D. (2000) *Social Work and Social Problems.* Basingstoke: Palgrave.

Smith, J.M. (1999) 'Prior criminality and employment of social workers with substantial access to children: A decision board analysis.' *British Journal of Social Work 29*, 1, 49–68.

Stanley, N. and Manthorpe, J. (2004) (eds) *The Age of Inquiry: Learning and Blaming in Health and Social Care.* London: Routledge

Stern, E. and Sommerlad, E. (1999) *Workplace Learning Culture and Performance.* London: IPD.

Stonewall (2010) *How to Engage Gay People in Your Work.* London: Stonewall.

Taylor, J., Williams, V., Johnson, R., Hiscutt, I. and Brennan, M. (2007) *We Are Not Stupid.* London: Shaping Our Lives and People First Lambeth.

Thomas, J.T., and Otis, M.D. (2010) 'Intrapsychic correlates of professional quality of life: Mindfulness, empathy, and emotional separation.' *Journal of the Society for Social Work and Research 1*, 2, 83–98.

Thompson, N. (2006) *People Problems.* Basingstoke: Palgrave Macmillan.

Tillet G. and French, B. (2006) *Resolving Conflict.* Oxford: Oxford University Press.

Tomm, K. (1988) *Interventive Interviewing: Part 111. Intending to Ask Lineal, Circular, Strategic, or Reflexive Questions? Family Process 27*, 1, 1–15

Van Eerde, W. (2003) 'Procrastination at work and time management training.' *Journal of Psychology 137*, 5, 1421–1434.

Virkus, S. (2003) 'Information literacy in Europe: A literature review.' *Information Research 8*, 4. Available at http://InformationR.net/ir/8-4/paper159.html, accessed October 2011.

Voice for the Child in Care (2004) *Start with the Child: Stay with the Child. Blueprint for a Childcentered Approach to Children and Young People in Public Care.* Available at www.voiceyp.org/ngen_public/default.asp?id=44, accessed October 2011.

Vygotsky, L.S. (1978) *Mind in Society.* Cambridge, MA: Harvard University Press.

Wallcroft, J. and Bryant, M. (2003) *The Mental Health Service User Movement in England.* London: Sainsbury Centre for Mental Health.

Walton, R.E. and McKersie, R.B. (1965) *A Behavioural Theory of Labor Negotiations.* London: McGraw-Hill.

Weinburg, A., Williamson, J., Challis, D. and Hughes, J. (2003) 'What do care managers do? A study of working practices in older people's services.' *British Journal of Social Work 33*, 7, 901–919.

Wheelan, S.A. (2010) *Creating Effective Teams: A Guide for Members and Leaders.* London: Sage.

Whitmore, J. (2009) *Coaching Performance.* London, Boston: Nicolas Brealey Publishing.

Wildridge, V., Childs, S., Cowthra, L. and Bruce, M. (2004) 'How to create successful partnerships – a review of the literature.' *Health Information and Libraries Journal 21*, 3–19.

Wright, P., Turner, Clay, D. and Mills, H. (2006) *The Participation of Children and Young People in Developing Social Care.* SCIE Guide 11. London: Social Care Institute for Excellence.

Zuboff, S. (1988) *In the Age of the Smart Machine: The Future of Work and Power.* New York: Basic Books.

Contributor Information

Christine Khisa is of Kenyan parentage and was born in London. She is a mother of four children and has used social care services for 25 years. Christine has participated in a variety of user involvement activities since 2005. She has been a 'link worker' on acute mental health wards and has co-delivered presentations with service users in training and education, within mental health as well as being employed as a Service User Involvement Co-ordinator, for both the South London and Maudsley Trust. Christine has participated in and delivered a specific 'train the trainers' course which equips service users with presentation and training skills.

In 2009 Christine piloted and managed, with support, a peer storytelling project in Lewisham, which is still ongoing. She is an active member of the user participation forums at Middlesex University and London South Bank University. She has been active in developing creative learning materials, using arts as a medium for dialogue and transition and has co-published and co-presented to various national forums on these projects.

Christine has a BSc in Social Sciences and at the time of writing she continues her studies towards a further qualification. Her personal interests are in articulating experiences through poetry, which she hopes to publish following writing poetry for various events and audiences. She also enjoys clothes design and is committed to promoting service user recovery and well-being through sharing experiences.

Subject Index

Author Index

Lightning Source UK Ltd.
Milton Keynes UK
UKOW04f0608070716

277788UK00002B/142/P